AWARD MONOLOGUES FOR WOMEN

The effectiveness of a performance is always influenced by the quality of the writing. We wanted to provide a treasure-house for actors of wonderful speeches with unique practical tips on how to perform them. We trust this collection of 54 monologues from plays nominated for:

* the Pulitzer Prize
* the Tony Award
* the Drama Desk Award
* the Evening Standard Theatre Award
* the Laurence Olivier Award

will help all of you who are looking for up-to-date speeches for auditions, acting class, or who just want to enjoy extracts from some of the new plays that have arrived in the last 25 years.

– Patrick Tucker and Christine Ozanne

Patrick Tucker is Director of the Original Shakespeare Company and author of *The Actor's Survival Handbook* (with Christine Ozanne, 2005), *Secrets of Screen Acting* (2nd edition, 2003) and *Secrets of Acting Shakespeare – the Original Approach* (2002).

Christine Ozanne is an actor, co-founder of the Original Shakespeare Company and co-author of *The Actor's Survival Handbook*.

AWARD MONOLOGUES FOR WOMEN

Edited by Patrick Tucker and Christine Ozanne

 Routledge
Taylor & Francis Group

LONDON AND NEW YORK

First published 2007 by Routledge
2 Park Square, Milton Park, Abingdon, Oxon OX14 4RN

Simultaneously published in the USA and Canada
by Routledge
270 Madison Ave, New York, NY 10016

Routledge is an imprint of the Taylor & Francis Group, an informa business

Typeset in Parisine by
Keystroke, 28 High Street, Tettenhall, Wolverhampton

Printed and bound in Great Britain by
TJ International Ltd, Padstow, Cornwall

British Library Cataloguing in Publication Data
A catalogue record for this book is available from the British Library

Library of Congress Cataloging in Publication Data
Award monologues for women / chosen and edited by Patrick
Tucker and Christine Ozanne.
    p. cm.
Includes bibliographical references and index.
1. Monologues. 2. Acting. 3. American drama—20th century.
4. English drama—20th century. 5. Women—Drama.
I. Tucker, Patrick. II. Ozanne, Christine.

PN2080.A97 2007
808.82'45—dc22   2007012605

ISBN10: 0–415–42839–4 (hbk)
ISBN10: 0–415–42840–8 (pbk)
ISBN13: 978–0–415–42839–2 (hbk)
ISBN13: 978–0–415–42840–8 (pbk)

Award Monologues for Women

Fifty-four speeches from plays that have won, or been nominated for, major Awards in New York and London from 1980 onwards; or from a performance by an actor similarly honoured

Chosen and edited by Patrick Tucker and Christine Ozanne

This book of various and varied speeches is dedicated to our various and varied siblings:

Martin, Nicholas, Elisabeth, Andrew and Gordon.

CONTENTS

INTRODUCTION

This book contains over 50 speeches.

These monologues are to help you:

1   to find a really good audition piece;
2   to find a suitable piece for classes which extend and improve your acting;
3   to find pieces that give you range and opportunity;
4   to see a selection of pieces from some well written plays.

SOURCES

Plays first presented since 1980, with the latest having its first performance in 2005.

WHICH

Those plays that have won or been nominated for major Theatre Awards in New York and London, or contain a speech performed by a similarly awarded actor. Two-thirds of the plays chosen are by American authors.

WHY AND HOW

We wanted all the speeches to come from well-written plays, and have read 328 of the 336 plays so nominated, plus most of the additional 199 plays that contain nominated performances. Because they are all plays connected with Awards, the writing is of a high standard – and we all know that the better the writing, the better your performance will be.

TEXT

We have reproduced the text exactly as it appears in the published script. Sometimes other characters have lines, but in all cases it is possible to perform the piece without someone else saying them.

DETAILS

The speeches are collected into four age-bands, and each speech has full details of when and where it was first performed and by whom, plus background details as to the character and situation.

NOTES

We have included specific notes and helpful hints at the bottom of each speech, along with definitions of any unusual words or references. There is a separate list of numbered notes for general use, and some Quick Advice on Auditioning.

LISTS

We have made a record of all the plays listed in the main New York and London Theatre Awards from 1980 to 2006, so you can see where the plays and playwrights come from, and when it was they received their accolades. We have also included an Index to all the plays used, plus all the individual actors who originally performed the speeches.

ACKNOWLEDGEMENTS

The idea and inspiration for these two related books (there is a companion volume *Award Monologues for Men*) comes from our long-time publisher and friend William Germano, who has been a constant supporter of our work.

Our editors at Routledge, Talia Rodgers and Minh Ha Duong, have been very helpful and supportive to the mammoth task of getting all the plays and permissions together.

Our research into the Award plays was mostly done at what we found to be the best source of play scripts in London, the library of the Royal Academy of Dramatic Art, whose staff were extremely helpful.

All the pieces in this volume are copyrighted, and the acknowledgements are given with each speech, where there are the details of who holds the copyright, and for which territory where appropriate. The holders of those rights wish to make it clear that you will need to seek permission for any public performance of these pieces, as well as any reproduction or photocopying of the work. The Owner's copyright in all these pieces shall be reserved

For the work of Israel Horovitz, professionals and amateurs are hereby warned that 'Park Your Car in Harvard Yard' being fully protected under the copyright laws of the United States of America, the British Commonwealth countries, including Canada, and the other countries of the Copyright Union, is subject to a royalty. All rights, including professional, amateur, motion picture, recitation, public reading, radio, television and cable broadcasting, and the rights of translation into foreign languages, are strictly reserved. Any inquiry regarding the availability of performance rights, or the purchase of individual copies of the authorized acting edition, must be directed to Samuel French Inc., 45 West 25 Street, NY, NY 10010 with other locations in Hollywood and Toronto, Canada.

For the work of Neil Simon, professionals and amateurs are hereby warned that 'Broadway Bound' and 'Lost in Yonkers' are fully protected under the Berne Convention and the Universal Copyright Convention and are subject to royalty. All rights, including without limitation professional, amateur, motion picture, television, radio, recitation, lecturing, public reading and foreign translation rights, computer media rights and the right of reproduction, and electronic storage or retrieval, in whole or in part and in any form, are strictly reserved and none of these rights can be exercised or used without written permission from the copyright owner. Inquiries for stock and amateur performances should be addressed to Samuel French Ltd., 52 Fitzroy Street, London W1P 6JR. All other inquiries should be addressed to Gary N. DaSilva, 111 N. Sepulveda Blvd., Suite 250, Manhattan Beach, CA 90266–6850, mail@garydasilva.com

HOW TO USE THIS BOOK

FIVE DIFFERENT WAYS OF FINDING A SPEECH:

1   Go to the **Contents** (page vii) to find the age bracket that suits you.
2   Go to the **Index of Playwrights** (page 141) to look up a specific writer.
3   Go to the **Index of Plays** (page 142) to look up a particular play.
4   Go to the **Index of Actors** (page 143) to look up what speech was originally performed by an actor similar to the type you are looking for.
5   Read through the speeches in your chosen age bracket to find the one that suits your purposes.

The text is as the author intended, with standardised stage instructions in italics inside square brackets. There has been no editing – all the other characters' lines are included, and the spelling (American or English) is as in the original text.

The speeches are arranged according to the age of the character: 20s, 30s, 40s, and over 50s, and then by alphabetical order of playwright. At the beginning of each section, all the speeches in that age range are listed.

DETAILS OF THE SPEECHES

At the top of each speech we name the author, and when it was first performed in a major city. The awards which the play or the performance gathered are listed, as is the character's name, and who first performed it. The age range for the character is listed according to the author (or failing further information, the age of the original actor who created the role), but these can often be just guidelines, and you should not feel restricted to looking only at those roles in your actual age range.

The type required for the part is stated, as well as a brief note as to the situation from where this speech comes. This is not gone into in great detail, as your performance will not be a re-creation of what you might do were you to be performing the role, but as a launch pad and platform for you to display all your acting abilities, and thrill the auditioners, and yourself, with the sheer joy of acting. A speech by itself cannot have the same effect as the same speech in the context of the play, and so it cannot be performed just as a slice of that play.

We have made a few comments at the bottom of each speech, including an explanation of any unusual words, and refer to the numbered **Notes on speeches** where applicable.

Although certain parts may be written for specific backgrounds of nationality, race or class, do not let this stop you from using one that will show YOU off to your best advantage, simply because you do not fit the exact requirements as asked for by the author.

QUICK ADVICE ON AUDITIONING

We as director (Patrick) and actor (Christine), have participated as performer and/or adjudicator in hundreds of classes, workshops, competitions, and auditions. Our advice and notes are drawn from these experiences.

1   The people judging you will be your 'audience' and need to be entertained as such.
2   If you need to announce the name of the piece you are doing, make it short: character, play title, author. There really shouldn't be any need to 'set the scene'. Exceptions should be only where appropriate, but whatever you do keep it brief and natural (not 'recited').
3   Start at once. Do not spend time getting into character; do not stand there with your eyes closed, breathing deeply and so on. Just get on with it. In other words, make an impact right from the start.
4   Use the simplest costume possible required for the character.
5   Use only those props that are absolutely necessary. Do not mix real props and mimed props in the same piece. Either one or the other.
6   Never apologize in advance for anything. Health problems, especially with the voice, will be obvious enough. *Never* give any hint that you don't know the piece very well, whatever the excuse might be. Again it will be obvious enough if you don't. If you have to take a prompt do it with aplomb, and don't come out of character. *Never re-run a line, just plough on regardless.* Chances are they won't notice your mistake if you do it with skill and confidence.
7   If you have to start again, either at their request or yours, try to do it differently to show what a flexible actor you are.
8   Be sensitive to the auditioners' remarks, don't argue a point, treat their comments as good advice.

9 Have an amusing anecdote ready if it refers to the audition piece, but only use it if you feel absolutely sure it will get a favourable reaction. Otherwise leave, quickly and cheerfully.

10 Before you begin, imagine that you have just done the audition and you are now going to do it even better!

NOTES ON SPEECHES

We realise that many of the notes we will be giving you will be repeated for different speeches, so instead of duplicating all the information onto each page, we give here all our main notes, numbered as **Note 1**, **Note 2**, etc. and then for each speech we will give some specific notes, followed by: **See Note 1**, **See Note 2** and so on, as appropriate.

NOTE 1   OTHER CHARACTER'S LINES

All the text is included. You can leave a gap where the other person is speaking, as it gives you a chance to do some good 'listening' acting. You can either act the information in the other lines, or add a few words so that the audience will know what it was that they were saying – such as putting them in the form of a question at the start of your next speech. A good alternative is to act the second character yourself, with a strong indication that this is what you are doing, such as using a change of voice. This can be a very effective short-cut to clarifying the other lines.

NOTE 2   LENGTH AND STYLE OF SPEECH

We have printed the speech up to a natural ending point, but it may be a little too long for your particular needs. Be unashamed in cutting a monologue down to suit those talents and abilities you wish to present or to work on – that is more important than presenting a coherent story.

NOTE 3   CONFUSING OR RUDE WORDS

Be happy to change any reference in the speech to one your audience will understand, such as place names or a specific cultural reference. If the language in the piece is inappropriate for your purposes (such as the use of profanities or swear words), then again be happy to change it.

NOTE 4 JOURNEY

Make sure your character goes on a journey, and that you end up in a different place to where you began. To stay the same leads an audience to wonder why they bothered to watch you, as you have not changed from first to last. If your character appears not to change in the speech, then make sure that the audience have gone on a learning journey as they watch your acting; someone must change, so if it is not you, then it must be the audience. Try not to be consistent – it is the enemy of good acting. If you hit one note and stay on it, the audience can easily guess the conclusion – and if they get there before you do it, it is a bored audience.

NOTE 5 THEORY OF OPPOSITES, AND SURPRISES

If you are to do something, do the opposite first. If you are about to be happy, then find a truthful way of being sad just before; if sad, then find a reason for your face to be smiling just before the 'sad' thought occurs. This will make the moment clearer and more fun for the audience to understand and enjoy. Also, try to find an unexpected way to deliver a line or certain word to surprise the audience. Let all interruptions catch you by 'surprise'. This is a good technique, especially at auditions.

NOTE 6 TALKING TO THE AUDIENCE

If you are alone on stage, then a few muttered words can be spoken as if to yourself – but a long speech never can: it is a soliloquy.

There are two schools of thought about how to deal with a soliloquy – you can either speak to a 'generalised' audience, never exactly catching anyone's eye, or you can speak to the audience directly. Some auditioners are uncomfortable if you include them in this, so if you plan to do so, check beforehand that this is going to be acceptable.

NOTE 7   ACCENTS AND VOICE

If the speech requires an accent which is not your natural one, be sure that you have a good reason for choosing it. Make sure you can sustain the accent effortlessly throughout, as any suspicion that you are not totally at ease with it will reflect badly in your performance, and good acting energy can be wasted on maintaining an accent. This also applies to 'character' voices that are not natural to you.

NOTE 8   STAGING

Always place the person you are speaking to downstage, so that when you talk to them the people watching you can see the changing thoughts on your face. If necessary, place chairs downstage of you to indicate where these other people will be.

NOTE 9   USE OF PROPERTIES (PROPS) AND COSTUMES

Either use real props, or mime them all. You do not have to have the exact prop, just something that will stand in for it. Doing a speech that leaves a broken prop onstage is not a good idea. An exception to mixing real and imaginary props is for food and drink, which are best mimed, for handling them when auditioning can be impractical. It is usually not a good idea to have a full costume, but an element of the correct one (a coat, a scarf, a hat) can be used to good effect.

20s

1

WILDEST DREAMS

Alan Ayckbourn

FIRST PERFORMANCES	Scarborough 1991; London 1993
AWARDS	Sophie Thompson nominated for the *Laurence Olivier Award for Best Actress in a Supporting Role*.
CHARACTER	Marcie
PLAYED BY	Rebecca Lacey; Sophie Thompson
CHARACTER'S AGE	early 20s
CHARACTER'S TYPE	She is attractive, fresh and untouched.
TIME AND PLACE	Today; the untidy basement of a large house in England.
SITUATION	Rick, as she likes to be known, lives in squalor in the basement of her house. Marcie has temporarily been given accommodation, as she is running away from a bullying husband.

Marcie: I – I might as well tell you. While you were out yesterday, I had a look upstairs . . . *[RICK looks at her sharply.]*

I'm sorry. I know you never want anyone to go up there but – well, it's such a waste, isn't it? It's vast. There's those three bedrooms and that huge sitting room and a lovely big bathroom. And the kitchen's huge. It's a lovely room. It could be. It's such a waste. Don't you think so, really? *[RICK does not reply.]*

I mean, I know it would need masses doing to it, but . . . We could really make it wonderful. Between us. It needn't cost a lot. It's all there. Basically. *[Silence.]*

I'm sorry. Are you very angry with me? Why can't you go up there? Is it – because of them? Your parents? Well, your mother and – But, Rick, darling, they've gone, haven't they? They're not there now. Are they part of the dreams you have? You do know you dream, don't you? Shout out in the night. You're always doing it. *[Laughing.]* I thought the house was on fire the first night you . . . *[Pause.]*

Actually, I must tell you – I had this awful fear that you'd . . . that they were – your parents were up there murdered or something. In a cupboard. You'd done them to death. There was this awful smell. But that just turned out to be the food. There was still this meal laid out – well, the remains of it – on the kitchen table. Was that the meal she left for you the day they . . .? Yes. Must have been. God! *[She shivers.]* Yes, I did, I read the note, as well. I'm sorry. I told you I'm a terribly nosy person. I didn't realize. Is that your real name? Alice? Alice. It's a lovely name. *[There is still no response from RICK. MARCIE suddenly stands.]*

Listen. Will you do something for me? For me? Will you? Come upstairs with me. Now. *[RICK looks at her again. MARCIE, holding out her hand.]*

Come on. Please. For me. Please. There's nothing there to be frightened of. No one. Trust me.

NOTES FOR THIS SPEECH:

You start off shy, but by the end you are dominant and in charge: **See Note 4**.

Use the 'Rick' to make us really believe you are speaking to a man, so that the surprise when you use the name 'Alice' will be all the more: **See Note 5**.

2

PAUL

Howard Brenton

FIRST PERFORMANCES	London 2005
AWARDS	Nominated for the *Laurence Olivier Award for Best New Play*.
CHARACTER	Mary Magdalene
PLAYED BY	Kellie Bright
CHARACTER'S AGE	25
TYPE	She is an uneducated young peasant girl.
TIME AND PLACE	AD 37; the house of James, brother of Yeshua.
SITUATION	Mary is talking to Paul, who is astounded to find that she was married to Yeshua.

Mary: *[MARY laughs.]* You really are one of 'em, aren't you? The 'God's sonners'.
Paul: The . . .
Mary: The lunatics who say Yeshua was God's son.
Paul: You of all people must know that He was.
Mary: Oh really? You think bed with him was some kind of mystical experience?
Paul: I . . .
Mary: Know why he married me? To spite his mother and father. They're rich, you know. Own just about the only business in Nazareth, employ half the village. Wood workshops. They're stuck up too: aristocratic blood, 'We are of the House of David' blah blah, they love all that. They saw Yeshua as High Priest one day, paid through the nose for him to be taught at the Temple in Jerusalem. Bright little kid he was too, they say. Knew the Torah off by heart. So when Yeshua took to the road with no shoes and a begging bowl, they weren't well pleased. Nothing

compared though, to when he married me. They didn't like that, not one bit. But he was over thirty so he could insist. His mother was in charge of the wedding party of course, so you know what she did? Served water. Yeshua had wine brought in. No, they didn't like it one bit, having a daughter-in-law who was a whore.

Paul: He married you to save you?

Mary: Yeah, he saved me. If he hadn't taken a liking to me, I'd be dead by now. Or good as, lying in a gutter outside a Roman barracks. *[Looks around nervously.]* I've got to go, they mustn't find me here.

NOTES FOR THIS SPEECH:

'God's sonners': those who believed that Yeshua (also called Jesus Christ) was the son of God.

You will need to act the other speeches, especially the last one, which could well be repeated by you: **See Note 1**.

There may well be some occasions or places where this speech would give offence: **See Note 3**.

3

BETTY'S SUMMER VACATION

Christopher Durang

FIRST PERFORMANCES	New York 1999
AWARDS	Nominated for the *Drama Desk Award for Outstanding Play*.
CHARACTER	Betty
PLAYED BY	Kellie Overbey
CHARACTER'S AGE	late 20s
TYPE	Sensible, does her best to be reasonable.
TIME AND PLACE	Now; night on the beach of a nice seaside community.
SITUATION	Betty went on vacation, and came across a house full of misfits, including voices in the ceiling, her friend Trudy and the owner Mrs Seizmagraff. Betty escaped just before the gas stove blew the house up.

Betty: *[Speedy, upset; partly to herself, partly to the audience.]* Where am I going to sleep tonight? I don't know why the people in the ceiling let me leave. I don't think I could have saved Mrs. Siezmagraff. I don't feel too guilty about it. I mean, they all seemed really terrible. I feel bad for Trudy, sort of . . . but well, I don't know what to think *[Looks out to the audience; includes them directly now.]* Now, actually, I think I'd like to become a hermit. Or I might become a nun if I could live in a convent in an isolated area with no other people around, and where no one in the convent is allowed to speak ever. I'd like that if it was quiet, and peaceful, and if they didn't care if I believed in God or not. *[Another idea.]* Or maybe I could start my own community where people don't speak. And we'd plant our own food, and we'd watch the birds in the trees. And maybe I'm having a breakdown. *[Holds the sides of her head, as if it might fly apart.]* Or is it a breakthrough? *[Hopeful; another possibility.]* Maybe it's a bad dream I had, and am still having. *[Looks around her.]* But I seem to be on the beach. And the house seems to be smoldering somewhere behind me in the distance. *[Looks behind her; the glow is almost out now; the sound of explosions has stopped; we hear the sound of the ocean.]* Isn't the sound of the ocean wonderful? *[Calming down slightly.]* What is it about it that sounds so wonderful? But it does. It makes me feel good. It makes me feel connected. *[Realizing what she said before was a little off.]* Well, maybe I don't have to join a convent where they don't speak. Maybe that's over-reacting. But it is hard to be around civilization. I don't like people. But there are nice people, though, aren't there? Yes. I'm sure you're very nice – although I'm just trying to ingratiate myself to you so you don't try to cut any of my body parts off. *[Laughs, then cries.]* Now I'm sad. *[Suddenly looks up, scared.]* Now I'm frightened. *[The emotions pass.]* No, now I'm fine. Listen to the ocean. That's why I wanted to come on this vacation, and have a summer share at the beach. I wanted to hear the ocean. But you know I forgot to listen to it the whole time I was with those people. But I'm going to listen to it now. *[Listens; she and the audience hear the sound of the waves; tension leaves BETTY's face and body.]* Oh that's lovely. Yes. Ocean, waves, sand. I'm starting to feel better. *[BETTY smiles at the audience. Closes her eyes. Continues to relax her body. Sound of the ocean continues. Lights dim.]*

NOTES FOR THIS SPEECH:

The more upset you are at the beginning, the greater the contrast will be when you settle down to sleep at the end: **See Note 4.**

Let each new idea of what you might become be different from the last one: **See Note 5.**

You are talking directly to the audience: **See Note 6.**

4

THE MARRIAGE OF BETTE AND BOO

Christopher Durang

FIRST PERFORMANCES	New York 1985
AWARDS	Nominated for the *Drama Desk Award for Outstanding New Play*.
	Joan Allen nominated for the *Drama Desk Award for Outstanding Actress in a Play*.
CHARACTER	Bette
PLAYED BY	Joan Allen
CHARACTER'S AGE	late 20s
CHARACTER'S TYPE	She is a fraught mother, after one birth and two miscarriages.
TIME AND PLACE	Now; Bette's home in America.
SITUATION	Bette is on the telephone, late at night, to an old schoolfriend.

Bette: Hello, Bonnie? This is Betsy. Betsy. *[To remind her.]* Bonnie, your grade is eight, and Betsy, your grade is five. Yes, it's me. How are you? Oh, I'm sorry, I woke you? Well, what time is it? Oh I'm sorry. But isn't Florida in a different time zone than we are? Oh. I thought it was. Oh well.

Bonnie, are you married? How many children do you have? Two. That's nice. Are you going to have any more? Oh, I think you should. Yes, I'm married. To Boo. I wrote you. Oh, I never wrote you? How many years since we've spoken? Since we were fifteen. Well, I'm not a very good correspondent. Oh, dear, you're yawning, I guess it's too late to have called. Bonnie, do you remember the beach and little Jimmy Winkler? I used to dress him up as a lamp shade, it was so cute. Oh. Well, do you remember when Miss Willis had me stand in the corner, and you stand in the wastebasket, and then your grandmother came to class that day? I thought you'd remember that. Oh, you want to go back to sleep?

Oh, I'm sorry. Bonnie, before you hang up, I've lost two babies. No, I don't mean misplaced, stupid, they died. I go through the whole nine-month period of carrying them, and then when it's over, they just take them away. I don't even see the bodies. Hello? Oh, I thought you weren't there. I'm sorry, I didn't realize it was so late. I thought Florida was Central Time or something, Yes, I got twelve in geography or something, you remember? Betsy, your grade is twelve and Bonnie, your grade is . . . what did you get in geography? Well, it's not important anyway. What? No, Boo's not home. Well, sometimes he just goes to a bar and then he doesn't come home until the bar closes, and some of them don't close at all and so he gets confused what time it is. Does your husband drink? Oh, that's good. What's his name? Scooter? Like bicycle? I like the name scooter. I love cute things. Do you remember Jackie Cooper in *Skippy* and his best friend Sukey? I cried and cried. Hello, are you still there? I'm sorry, I guess I better let you go back to sleep. Good-bye, Bonnie, it was good to hear your voice. *[Hangs up.]*

NOTES FOR THIS SPEECH:

'Skippy': Jackie Cooper at the age of 10 was nominated in 1931 for an Oscar for his role in this film, where he tries to save his friend's dog.

It will be fun to create the other character at the end of the phone, and give her a real presence.

Obviously she does not remember the past as well as you do, and this will allow you to build up, then deflate your emotions: **See Note 5**.

5

CRIMES OF THE HEART

Beth Henley

FIRST PERFORMANCES	Louisville 1979; New York 1981; London 1983
AWARDS	Won *The Pulitzer Prize for Drama*; nominated for the *Drama Desk Award for Outstanding New Play*, and the *Tony Award for Best Play*.
	Mia Dillon nominated for the *Tony Award for Best Actress in a Featured Role in a Play*.
	Mary Beth Hurt [US: Meg] nominated for the *Tony Award for Best Actress in a Featured Role in a Play* and the *Drama Desk Award for Outstanding Actress in a Play*.
CHARACTER	Babe
PLAYED BY	Lee Anne Fahey, Mia Dillon [US]; Wendy Morgan [UK]
CHARACTER'S AGE	24
CHARACTER'S TYPE	She is a Mississippi girl, with an angelic face, and fierce volatile eyes; a bit dim-witted and a sugar-holic.
TIME AND PLACE	Now; Hazlehurst, Mississippi, at the home of her grandfather.
SITUATION	Babe is out on bail after shooting her husband Zackery in the stomach, and is talking to her sister Meg about how her affair with a 15-year-old black boy led to the shooting.

Babe: Well, I'm not! I'm not a liberal! I'm a democratic! I was just lonely! I was so lonely. And he was good. Oh, he was so, so good. I'd never had it that good. We'd always go out into the garage and –

Meg: It's okay, I've got the picture; I've got the picture! Now, let's just get back to the story. To yesterday, when you shot Zackery.

Babe: All right, then. Let's see . . . Willie Jay was over. And it was after we'd –

Meg: Yeah! Yeah.

Babe: And we were just standing around on the back porch playing with Dog. Well, suddenly, Zackery comes from around the side of the house. And he startled me 'cause he's supposed to be away at the office, and there he is coming from 'round the side of the house. Anyway, he says to Willie Jay, 'Hey, boy, what are you doing back here?' And I said, 'He's not doing anything. You just go on home, Willie Jay! You just run right on home.' Well, before he can move, Zackery comes up and knocks him once right across the face and then shoves him down the porch steps, causing him to skin up his elbow real bad on that hard concrete. Then he says, 'Don't you ever come around here again, or I'll have them cut out your gizzard!' Well, Willie Jay starts crying, these tears come streaming down his face, then he gets up real quick and runs away with Dog following off after him. After that, I don't remember much too clearly; let's see . . . I went on into the living room, and I went right up to the davenport and opened the drawer where we keep the burglar gun . . . I took it out. Then I – I brought it up to my ear. That's right. I put it right inside my ear. Why, I was gonna shoot off my own head! That's what I was gonna do. Then I heard the back door slamming and suddenly, for some reason, I thought about mama . . . how she'd hung herself. And here I was about ready to shoot myself. Then I realized – that's right I realized how I didn't want to kill myself! And she – she probably didn't want to kill herself. She wanted to kill him, and I wanted to kill him, too. I wanted to kill Zackery, not myself. 'Cause I – I wanted to live! So I waited for him to come on into the living room. Then I held out the gun, and I pulled the trigger, aiming for his heart, but getting him in the stomach. *[After a pause.]* It's funny that I really did that.

'gizzard': intestines, innards;

'davenport': small writing desk.

You will need to let us know what your sister says to you: **See Note 1**.

Get really involved in your memories of the good times with Willie, in order to snap out of it abruptly. Also, for a surprise, you could end by laughing: **See Note 5**.

It will help you act the other conversations if you place your sister down stage of you: **See Note 8**.

6

CLEO, CAMPING, EMMANUELLE AND DICK

Terry Johnson

FIRST PERFORMANCES	London 1998
AWARDS	**Won** the *Laurence Olivier Award for Best New Comedy*.
CHARACTER	Imogen
PLAYED BY	Gina Bellman
CHARACTER'S AGE	late 20s
CHARACTER'S TYPE	She is an attractive actress, drunk and not as vivacious as she was.
TIME AND PLACE	1969; outside the famous comedy actor Sid James' trailer on a British film set.
SITUATION	Sid has just finished 'learning his lines' with Imogen, an aspiring actress.

Imogen: I'm surprised you even remembered me. I'm flattered. I mean, who was I then? I was out and about, I know, but I'd barely left LAMDA and honestly I knew nothing. I *was* nothing. This is such a strange business. You get a job, you meet someone, you like them, you maybe sleep with them, the job ends, then you never see them again even though you always say you will. I made some really good friends on *When Dinosaurs Ruled the Earth*, except Raquel of course, but she doesn't make friends she just takes the odd hostage. Thing is I haven't seen anyone since. Except there was a particularly persistent caveman who I did see once but his wife was pregnant and he just cried all evening. Everything's so . . . temporary. That's what's nice about working with you lot;

you're one big happy family. I'd love to work with you lot again. *[IMOGEN carries on drinking.]*

Sid: I'm gonna be needed soon.

Imogen: Oh, that's all right; I only popped in to say hello. You know what I wish? I wish I had smaller breasts. Then I'd get to play some women with small breasts, and they're always the best parts. I'd really like to play women with no breasts at all, you know, like in Ibsen. I should never have done the centerfold. I'm actually very versatile. 'An impressive multifaceted performance'; that's what they said about me as Jenny Grubb in *Loving*. And that wasn't just taking off the glasses and letting my hair down, that was *acting* actually. I was *acting* her repressed sexually. What I'm saying is, I'm not just some stupid girl from Elmhurst with a fucked knee, you know. I'm not just the Countess of Cleavage; all right? It's so hard to convince people I'm a serious actress, but I really think it's beginning to happen. I've got an audition for the Royal Shakespeare Company? And last month I did *The Persuaders*. Only the pilot but both Roger Moore *and* Tony Curtis were very complimentary and said there was a very good chance my character could become a regular.

NOTES FOR THIS SPEECH:

'LAMDA': one of the top drama schools in the UK;

'*When Dinosaurs Ruled the Earth*': film starring Raquel Welch;

'Elmhurst'. ballet school in England;

'*The Persuaders*': television series starring Roger Moore and Tony Curtis.

It is easy to act the other character's line: See Note 1.

You may want to change some of the words, or update the film references: See Note 3.

Be happy to remember the persistent caveman, in order to have the bigger gear change when you talk of his wife: See Note 5.

Although it is set in England, you can use any accent for this piece: See Note 7.

It would be easier to use a real glass: See Note 9.

7

HITCHCOCK BLONDE

Terry Johnson

FIRST PERFORMANCES	London 2003; Costa Mesa 2006
AWARDS	Nominated for the *Laurence Olivier Award for Best New Play*.
CHARACTER	Blonde
PLAYED BY	Rosamund Pike [UK]; Sarah Aldrich [US]
CHARACTER'S AGE	early 20s
CHARACTER'S TYPE	She is a blonde, attractive working actress, with an abusive husband.
TIME AND PLACE	1959; a small kitchen in America.
SITUATION	The actress who was the stand-in for the filming of the bath-tub murder scene in *Psycho* describes what happened on the day.

Blonde: So the First shouts, 'Turn over!', and the Jewish guy, so quietly, says, 'Action.' Hah. This'll make you laugh. The props guy with the knife raises it and as he does, he did the most remarkable thing. He *looked away*. It's a real knife, it's real close and he looks away. I couldn't help it, I stepped backwards, out of focus, out of the light, I wrecked the shot. 'Cut!' shouts the First, 'What's the problem?' 'He looked away.' 'I what?' 'You looked away. Do me a favour. Don't look away.' So that was it. Permission granted. The naked lady.

Oh, the coffee break. Nowhere to put my cup. Nowhere to sit without clambering out which meant bending one leg and I don't think so. So I was in that tub the entire afternoon. I was cold. And I was stiff. And by four o'clock, not looked at. They had seen more than enough of me by then, they'd had their fill.

As we called a wrap, the dresser was somewhere else and the robe was hanging on a peg like thirty yards away, so I just hopped out of the tub and ducked under a lamp and smiled at the gaffer who smiled back and just stepped through coils of thick cable and walked those thirty yards past standbys packing up and the caterers wrapping the coffee; the nude lady heading for her robe and something in me didn't care if I never got there. Then I put on the robe and I felt like no one. I went to the restaurant my husband manages and I found the waitress he was screwing. I poured coffee on her. It wasn't hot. He whacked me with the heel of his hand. Why he likes doing that I've no idea. You'd think he'd break his wrist but no, he just liked using the heel of his hand. I went down. He kicked me in the hip. He threw me in a cab. He went back to help the waitress with her blouse. I drank a Jack Daniel's. I drank more Jack Daniel's. He came home.

NOTES FOR THIS SPEECH:

'First': another term for the Assistant Director;

'Jewish guy': Saul Bass did the story boards for the *Psycho* shower sequence, and was alleged to have directed some of the shots;

'wrap': announces the end of that day's filming;

'gaffer': chief electrician;

'Jack Daniel's': American bourbon (whisky).

Since she is an actress, she would act the other characters well.

Make sure 'not looked at' is a real gear change and surprise for the audience: See Note 5.

You are talking to the audience: See Note 6.

8

LOBBY HERO

Kenneth Lonergan

FIRST PERFORMANCES	New York 2001; London 2002
AWARDS	Nominated for the *Drama Desk Award for Outstanding Play*, and the *Laurence Olivier Award for Best New Comedy*.
	David Tennant [UK: Jeff] nominated for the *Laurence Olivier Award for Best Actor*.
CHARACTER	Dawn
PLAYED BY	Heather Burns [US]; Charlotte Randle [UK]
CHARACTER'S AGE	early 20s
CHARACTER'S TYPE	She is a rookie cop.
TIME AND PLACE	Now; the security officer's room in a New York apartment building.
SITUATION	Investigating a murder, she discovers from Jeff the security guard that her police partner Bill has been two-timing her, and that Jeff himself is in love with her.

Dawn: I'm not in love with anybody. I just admired him, that's all. OK? He made life a little easier for me in the Department. OK? I mean, you look up to somebody, you take them seriously – and then – that's all. OK?

Jeff: OK. I think it's great what you are doing. Your family must be proud of you.

Dawn: Oh, they think I'm nuts. *[Pause.]* Well, not exactly, I mean, my mother thinks I'm a little bit nuts, but I happen to think that she's nuts too, so there's no harm done there, right?

Jeff: You have a lot of brothers? I bet you have a lot of –

Dawn: But I guess generally they're proud . . . I was near the top of my class at the Academy . . . I just . . . I just fucked up with *this* prick, that's all. And now I'm *screwed*. Because I obviously really misjudged him, you know? And for all I know he's been shootin' his mouth off all over the Department. And it wouldn't have been so hard to avoid the whole thing in the first place. But these guys . . . I mean, they seen so much horrible shit, it's like they don't give a damn about anything. So you gotta walk around like you don't give a damn about anything either. But they know you still do. And they wanna like, stamp it out of you or something. And like, test you, all the time. And it's always like: 'Hey – you're not men, you're not women: You're cops. Act like cops and you'll be treated like cops.' Only then it turns out they got a pool going as to who's gonna fuck you first, OK? And that's fine. I can handle it. You *make* them respect you. But then somebody decent comes along, and goes out of his way to make life easier for you – and I didn't even *ask* him, because I didn't expect anything different – I didn't *want* anything different. And then, Oh my God, it's true love – except when he comes down in that elevator, just watch: because *I'm* gonna be the one who's gonna be supposed to act like I'm a cop! I mean . . . *[Pause.]* And then I got *you*.

NOTES FOR THIS SPEECH:

You need to help the audience understand what is said to you by Jeff: **See Note 1**.

You may need to change some of the words: **See Note 3**.

Your mood will change a lot from talking about being a cop to talking about your partner: **See Note 5**.

9

RECKLESS

Craig Lucas

FIRST PERFORMANCES	New York 1988, 2004
AWARDS	Nominated for the *Drama Desk Award for Outstanding New Play*.
CHARACTER	Fourth Doctor
PLAYED BY	Joyce Reehling, Debra Monk
CHARACTER'S AGE	late 20s
CHARACTER'S TYPE	She is a young doctor; but could be any age.
TIME AND PLACE	Today; a consulting Doctor's office.
SITUATION	The doctor is trying to help her patient with 'birth therapy', of getting her to experience again the trauma of being born.

Fourth Doctor: This is very important, Cheryl. We've talked about the birth scream. It is a terrible shock to be torn away in a shower of blood with your mother screaming and your home torn open and the strange doctor with his rubber hands slapping you with all his might and the cold light piercing the dark, the warm beautiful wet dark, the silent murmuring safe dark of Mummy everywhere and Daddy, everything is one and everything is sex and we are all together for eternity and we are happy and nothing ever passes through your mind but good thoughts until suddenly this squeezing is going on around you and everyone is pushing and pulling and cold steel tongs pinch your skin and pull you by the top of your head and you don't want to go, no, you don't want to leave your home where you're always floating in and your mother's heart is always beating for something unknown and cruel where people are cold and you're stinging now, everything is breaking, it makes you want to scream, Cheryl, makes you want to scream the scream of all ages, scream of the greatest tragedy of all time and your mummy is screaming and your daddy is screaming and now all the doctors are screaming and everything's blinding you and you're torn away and they're hitting you and they throw you up in the air and you open your eyes and your mother is covered in blood and you scream, Cheryl, scream, scream, *scream*, Cheryl, SCREAM, *SCREAM!!! [Pause.]*

All right, we'll try it again.

NOTES FOR THIS SPEECH:

Really assume that she is going to come up with a big scream during the pause, which will give you a nice 'down-to-earth' effect for your last line: **See Note 5.**

You could start the speech sitting, placing Cheryl downstage of you, and as the scene builds, get up so that you are really trying to intimidate her at the end: **See Note 8.**

You could always put on a white doctor's coat: **See Note 9.**

10

RECKLESS

Craig Lucas

FIRST PERFORMANCES	New York 1988, 2004
AWARDS	Nominated for the *Drama Desk Award for Outstanding New Play*.
	Robin Bartlett [1988: Rachel] nominated for the *Drama Desk Award for Outstanding Actress in a Play*.
	Mary-Louise Parker [2004: Rachel] nominated for the *Tony Award for Best Actress in a Play*.
CHARACTER	Pooty
PLAYED BY	Welker White, Rosie Perez
CHARACTER'S AGE	23 – 24
CHARACTER'S TYPE	She is a paraplegic, short and stout, in a wheelchair.
TIME AND PLACE	Today; Lloyd's living room, somewhere in America.
SITUATION	Rachel is being given refuge for a while by Lloyd, whose girlfriend Pooty speaks to Rachel for the first time and tells her the truth about herself: that she is pretending to be deaf and dumb to impress her lover.

Pooty: Now, listen, he can't know. *[RACHEL is dumbfounded.]* It would break his heart. . . . I'm sorry I didn't say anything before.

Rachel: Oh, listen . . . you know.

Pooty: When I lost the use of my legs a friend drove me up here to Springfield to take a look at this place where they worked with the handicapped. I watched the physical therapists working with the patients and there was one: I remember he was working with a quadriplegic. I thought he was the most beautiful man I'd ever seen. A light shining out through his skin. And I thought if I couldn't be with him I'd die. But I knew I would just be one more crippled dame as far as he was concerned, so my friend helped to get me registered as deaf and disabled. I used to teach sign language to the hearing impaired. I thought if I were somehow needier than the rest I would get special attention. I realized soon enough: everyone gets special attention where Lloyd is concerned. But by then it was too late. He was in love with me, with my honesty. He learned to sign; he told me how he'd run away from a bad marriage and changed his name so he wouldn't have to pay child support. He got me a job at Hands Across the Sea and I couldn't bring myself to tell him that I had another name and another life, that I'd run away too, because I owed the government so much money and wasn't able to pay after the accident. I believe in honesty. I believe in total honesty. And I need him and he needs me to be the person he thinks I am and I am that person, I really am that person. I'm a crippled deaf girl, short and stout. Here is my wheelchair, here is my mouth.

Rachel: I'm not judging you.

Pooty: When he goes out I babble. I recite poetry I remember from grade school. I talk back to the television. I even call people on the phone and say it's a wrong number just to have a conversation. I'm afraid I'm going to open my mouth to scream one day and . . . *[She does; no sound.]*

NOTES FOR THIS SPEECH:

You might like the option, before you sit down to start the speech, of establishing with your audience that Pooty has been pretending to be deaf and dumb.

Rachel's first speech is her astonishment that you can talk; her second one is easy for you to act: **See Note 1.**

Since you are not used to speaking, it would be nice for you to start with your voice a bit rusty, and get more fluent as you speak more. Lots of varieties will help the speech: **See Note 4.**

You can use a simple chair as the wheelchair, and you should put Rachel downstage of you: **See Note 8.**

11

THE DEAD EYE BOY

Angus MacLachlan

FIRST PERFORMANCES	Cincinnati 2000; New York 2001; London 2002
AWARDS	Lili Taylor nominated for the *Drama Desk Award for Outstanding Actress in a Play*.
	Aaron Himelstein [US: Soren] nominated for the *Drama Desk Award for Outstanding Actor in a Play*.
CHARACTER	Shirley
PLAYED BY	Raye Lankford; Lili Taylor [US]; Nicola Walker [UK]
CHARACTER'S AGE	29
CHARACTER'S TYPE	She is physically tiny with a rough voice that sounds like she was yelling all day yesterday. An addict.
TIME AND PLACE	The present; North Carolina. A Counselor's Office.
SITUATION	Shirley is at the Counselor's with her 14-year-old son Soren. At the start of the session, Soren tears up his composition book. Shirley tries to be attentive, but is completely high on drugs, thinking no one can tell.

Shirley: You gonna give it to me?

Soren: If you want.

Shirley: I want it. Let me see. *[He gives her a folded up piece of paper.]* Is it good? Will I like it? Is it funny? *[Reads.]* 'Rough Life, my story by Soren Horace Watts.' *[She glances at him. Lightly mocking.]* Ohhh. *[He smiles. She smiles.]* 'Once there was a kid named Soren Horace. His mother was Shirley-Diane Watts. She got raped at the age of fourteen by some body, who knows who?' *[She takes a small* *pause, but doesn't look up, and keeps reading.]* 'That's how she got pregnant with Soren. The kid blamed hisself 'cause she would have forgot if he never was alive. When I look in the mirror I see the Dead Eye Boy. The reason his eye was like that is 'cause his mom got raped and what happened in childbirth. That's what looks back at me when I see myself. What will happen to the Dead Eye Boy I don't know. But he won't be around for long, that's for sure. The end.' *[SHIRLEY stares at the paper.]* It should be himself. Hisself isn't a word. *[She looks at the COUNSELOR.]* Right? *[She waits.]* Is that what you think? *[SOREN doesn't say anything.]* Is it? *[She waits.]* Is that, like, what you're telling me here? *[Referring to him tearing up the notebook.]* Like, why you're doing that there? *[She waits.]* When I told you all that I was messed up, I shouldn't – I didn't mean for you . . . Listen, what happened to me was my business and it doesn't have anything to do with you. You know – I think of it, like, it happened to another person even. *[He shrugs his shoulders.]* It's dead and buried and forgotten. So it's nothing for you to worry about. *[She pauses – fighting away something deep. And managing to.]* And, if you wasn't wanted. Well, hell – um – I mean – You know about abortions? You know what they are. You're smart. Do you think that wasn't an option? I could have. My mother – But, I didn't. 'Cause I thought . . . Or – god – Don't you know about adoption? . . . *You* know. *[He doesn't speak.]* I kept you 'cause I wanted you 'cause I loved you you were mine. You were somebody for *me* to have. You were mine to keep. *[She waits.]* I made a decision. At that time. *[She turns out towards the COUNSELOR.]* Trying to make something good to come out of something bad. *[Pause.]* You know? I was raped. I was fourteen. *[Pause.]* It was my choice. I thought. Back then . . . Then I forgot all about it . . . That's it. *[She shakes her head.]* Anyway, he knows the truth.

NOTES FOR THIS SPEECH:

The height and voice description by the author does not, of course, have to apply to you.

Act the missing speech: **See Note 1.**

Even though you are high, avoid doing the whole speech on one note: **See Note 4.**

Place your son and your counsellor downstage and to each side of you, so you can clearly act which one you are talking to, or talking about: **See Note 8.**

You could use a real piece of paper to read as a prop: **See Note 9.**

12

OLEANNA

David Mamet

FIRST PERFORMANCES	New York 1992; London 1992
AWARDS	Nominated for the *Drama Desk Award for Outstanding New Play*, and for the *Laurence Olivier Award for Best New Play*.
	David Suchet [UK: John] nominated for the *Laurence Olivier Award for Best Actor*.
CHARACTER	Carol
PLAYED BY	Rebecca Pidgeon [US]; Lia Williams [UK]
CHARACTER'S AGE	20
TYPE	An intense student.
TIME AND PLACE	Now; the rooms of a university lecturer.
SITUATION	The professor has been condescending to his student, and she has reported him for sexual harassment. Each is sure of the rightness of their case: he that putting his hand on her shoulder was comforting; she that it was harassment.

Carol: Professor. I came here as a *favor*. At your personal request. Perhaps I should not have done so. But I did. On my behalf, and on behalf of my group. And you speak of the tenure committee, one of whose members is a woman, as you know. And though you might call it Good Fun, or An Historical Phrase, or An Oversight, or, All of the Above, to refer to the committee as Good Men and True, it is a demeaning remark. It is a sexist remark, and to overlook it is to countenance continuation of that method of thought. It's a remark . . .

John: OH COME ON. Come on . . . Sufficient to deprive a family of . . .

Carol: Sufficient? Sufficient? Sufficient? Yes. It is a *fact* . . . and that story, which I quote, is *vile* and *classist*, and *manipulative* and *pornographic*. It . . .

John: . . . it's pornographic . . .?

Carol: What gives you the *right*. Yes. To speak to a *woman* in your private . . . Yes. Yes. I'm sorry. I'm sorry. You feel yourself empowered . . . you say so yourself. To *strut*. To *posture*. To 'perform.' To 'Call me in here . . .' Eh? You say that higher education is a joke. And treat it as such, you *treat* it as such. And *confess* to a taste to play the *Patriarch* in your class. To grant *this*. To deny *that*. To embrace your students.

John: How can you assert. How can you stand there and . . .

Carol: How can you *deny* it. You did it to me. *Here*. You *did*. . . . You *confess*. You love the Power. To *deviate*. To *invent*, to transgress . . . to *transgress* whatever norms have been established for us. And you think it's charming to 'question' in yourself this taste to mock and destroy. But you should question it. Professor. And you pick those things which you feel *advance* you: publication, *tenure*, and the steps to get them you call 'harmless rituals.' And you perform those steps. Although you say it is hypocrisy. But to the aspirations of your students. Of *hard-working students*, who come here, who *slave* to come here – you have no idea what it cost me to come to this school – you *mock* us. You call education 'hazing,' and from your so-protected, so-elitist seat you hold our confusion as a *joke*, and our hopes and efforts with it. Then you sit there and say 'what have I done? And ask me to understand that *you* have aspirations too. But I tell you. I tell you. That you are vile. And that you are exploitative. And if you possess one ounce of that inner honesty you describe in your book, you can look in yourself and see those things that I see. And you can find revulsion equal to my own. Good day.

NOTES FOR THIS SPEECH:

The other conversations can either be acted, or in fact spoken by you: **See Note 1.**

You are working up to making a grand exit, so you will need to start small, in order to get the maximum build: **See Note 4.**

Make sure you place him in a good position for you: **See Note 8.**

13

BOMBSHELLS

Joanna Murray-Smith

FIRST PERFORMANCES	Melbourne 2001; London 2004
AWARDS	Caroline O'Connor nominated for the *Laurence Olivier Award for Best Actress*.
CHARACTER	Theresa
PLAYED BY	Caroline O'Connor [Australia and UK]
CHARACTER'S AGE	20
CHARACTER'S TYPE	She is an enthusiastic bride-to-be.
TIME AND PLACE	Now; during a wedding service in church.
SITUATION	A bride is in her wonderful wedding dress, having second thoughts, speaking to the audience as she is being married to Ted.

Theresa: Here we go. Here we go. What's Ted saying? What's Ted saying? *We should never have written our own vows!* 'I promise to nurture you like a small sapling growing beside the mighty river of love. I promise to water you and dispense sunlight over you and allow you to grow into a – *[Beat. Trying to get her mouth around it:]* Large. Sturdy. Trunk.' – The vicar looks kind of sexy in that outfit – 'I promise to grow beside you and protect you from the elements of life and to provide companionship to you as we become part of the forest of togetherness.' *[Back to interior reality.]*

Do vicars have sex? In just a couple of seconds I will never be able to have sex with this vicar or any other living man. *Or dead.* Living or dead. They're all totally off the cards. They're gone, they're over, they're not even a blip on the radar. From now on it's me and the girls down one end of the table talking about George

Clooney, and Ted and the boys down the other talking about stock options. Do you love Ted, Theresa? Do you regret it? Do you regret it? Do you regret it? *[Beat.]* I do. *[Beat. Quietly:]* What have I done? *[Beat. Quietly:]* What have I done? *[Beat.]* *I only really wanted to wear the dress.* The dress. The dress. It's all about the dress. *[Beat. Building in volume and speed:]*

Outside the maths room. Me and Leanne Snowball talking about the dress the dress the dress. When Ted asked, when he turned to me, straight away I thought, I thought: The dress! The dress! And telling Mum. Mum cried. She put her hands flat on on her cheeks. Mum yelled: The dress! When I told the girls – I told the girls – they cried. The dress! The dress! It's all about the dress! Plunging neckline, high neck, sweetheart, strapless, slim-fitting, loose-fitting, layered, netted, textured, embroidered, beaded, cream, white, ivory, gold, glacial, elegant, striking, imaginative, a triumph, a triumph, a triumph! *It's all about the dress!*

'You may – ?' 'You may – ?' What's he – ? What's he – ? 'You may kiss' – 'You may kiss' . . . *[Dawning on her:]* The bride.

IT'S THE DRESS'S FAULT. The dress is to blame. The dress is to blame. I'M SUING THE DRESS!

NOTES FOR THIS SPEECH:

There are two focuses here: the ceremony marrying you to Ted, and your relationship with the audience. Make sure you are clear which you are addressing; and that the audience enjoy the contrast in your relationships with the two: See Note 4.

Because 'the dress' is repeated so many times, find as many different ways of saying it as possible; don't let the audience guess how the next one will come out: See Note 5.

This is a soliloquy: See Note 6.

This piece is clearly set in Australia. The accent would bring out the colloquial humour: See Note 7.

It is obviously impossible to wear a complete wedding dress; you could just wear a bit of white on your head: See Note 9.

14

BUICKS

Julian Sheppard

FIRST PERFORMANCES	New York 2003
AWARDS	**Won** the *Drama Desk Award for Outstanding Play*.
	Norbert Leo Butz [Bill] nominated for the *Drama Desk Award for Outstanding Actor in a Play*.
CHARACTER	Naranja
PLAYED BY	Lucia Brawley
CHARACTER'S AGE	22
CHARACTER'S TYPE	She is a Mexican immigrant, and works as a receptionist.
TIME AND PLACE	Today; a motel room near Albuquerque.
SITUATION	Bill Abeline's wife has left him and his Car Dealership, and he has gone looking for her accompanied by his receptionist. She is showing her boss how she would sell a car.

Naranja: Do you . . . do you like this model?

Bill: Yeah, sure, whatever.

Naranja: No whatever, sir. I tell you secret, you not tell anybody. The Park Avenue is easily my favorite model of all the cars on the lot. Do you know why? I bet you know what I am thinking . . .

Bill: No . . .

Naranja: It is the strongest-looking of all the cars on the lot. It has a style. People, they often say, Buicks, not a stylish car. But this model – I think it really has a *flair*. And you would look exceptional driving it. You would look . . . strong.

Bill: Hm. You think?

Naranja: Absolutely. And it is not just that it has this style. I feel it is the car which is right for you. Let me tell you why. Power and comfort. This is what the Park Avenue has. Power. Comfort. I see that you are a man who need the extra horse-power you can only get with the special supercharged V-6 engine that come with the Park Avenue. You would like to have that little extra kick, yes, who would not?

Bill: Yeah, a little power'd be good.

Naranja: But you also need the extra comfort – the extra *luxury* of the Park Avenue. Ten-way power front seats – you, as you should – would have absolute control. This feature only comes in our Park Avenue. Also available in our Ultra package, only in the Park Avenue, are heated front seats with lumbar adjustment. You and your lovely wife – what is your wife's name?

Bill: Millicent.

Naranja: You and Millicent are taking a long drive on a beautiful chilly winter night. It is romantic. You feel in control of the road with your four-speed automatic transmission, your antilock four-wheel disc brakes, your supercharged 3.8 liter V-6 engine. You and your wife are comfortable. But you are . . . a little cold. And your back is a little stiff. You are a tall man. You need space for breathing. In the Park Avenue, you have the highest combination of front leg room and head of any our spacious Buick models. You would ride in great comfort, with great power at your fingertips. The Ultra package, which I am sure you would be interested in, goes for merely thirty-eight thousand one hundred dollars. I think one test drive will suffice to show you that the Buick Park Avenue is the best car for you. Shall we take spin, or wait for your lovely wife, Millicent?

NOTES FOR THIS SPEECH:

Bill makes the simple obvious responses in his speeches: **See Note 1**.

Allow the confidence in your ability to sell a car grow, so that you start at one level, and end on a very different one: **See Note 4**.

Because we don't hear him say his wife's name, maybe you are surprised by it? A slight pause before choosing 'Millicent' is unexpected; it is also the last word of the piece: See Note 5.

Only do the accent if you are good at it: **See Note 7**.

You could get very flirtatious (the way super salesgirls are) on the last paragraph, if you imagine he is in a chair downstage of you, and you are working on him from behind, whispering in his ear: **See Note 8**.

15
PTERODACTYLS

Nicky Silver

FIRST PERFORMANCES	New York 1993
AWARDS	Nominated for the *Drama Desk Award for Outstanding Play*.
	Hope Davis nominated for the *Drama Desk Award for Outstanding Supporting Actress in a Play*.
CHARACTER	Emma
PLAYED BY	Hope Davis
CHARACTER'S AGE	20
CHARACTER'S TYPE	She was a hypochondriac with memory problems, now she is dead.
TIME AND PLACE	Now; Duncan family home, in the American suburbs.
SITUATION	Emma had brought her fiancé Tommy home, and during the wedding preparations he fell in love with her brother Todd. She has shot herself with the wedding present from her brother, and Tommy now is also dead.

Emma: Hello everybody. I'm dead. How are you? I'm glad I killed myself. I'm not recommending it for others, mind you – no Dr. Kevorkian am I. But it's worked out for me. Looking back, I don't think I was ever supposed to have been born to begin with. Of course the idea that anything is 'supposed to be' implies a master plan, and I don't believe in that kind of thing.

When I say I shouldn't have been born, I mean that my life was never all that pleasant. And there was no real reason for it. I was pretty. I had money. I was lucky enough to be born in a time and into a class where I had nothing but opportunities. I look around and there are crippled people and blind people and refugees and I can't believe I had the gall to whine about anything! I had my health

– oh sure, I complained a lot, but really I was fine. And I had love! Granted the object of my affections was a latent, or not-so-latent homosexual as it turned out, who was infected with the HIV virus, who in turn infected me and my unborn baby – but isn't that really picking nits?

I can never thank Todd enough for giving me the gun, because for the first time, I'm happy. The pain is gone and I remember everything. Tommy is here, but we're not speaking. He spends all his time with Montgomery Clift and George Cukor talking about movies. I assume.

And I've been reunited with Alice Paulker. We went to school together. She was shot last year by a disgruntled postal worker. She has long, wavy brown hair and skin so pale you can see right through it – I don't mean it's really transparent and you can see her guts and organs and everything. It's just pale. And she has very big eyes, green. And we listen to music and go for walks. We take turns reading aloud to each other. She reads poems by Emily Bronte and I read chapters from *The Tropic of Cancer* by Henry Miller. She was always classier than me. And sometimes, we don't read. Sometimes, we just hold each other. And I run my fingers through her hair and she touches her lips, gently, along my cheek. She makes soft sounds, comforting sounds and she takes her time and she runs her tongue along the edge of my ear. We take off our clothes and just look at each other. I was shy at first, but Alice helped me and never rushed me. She held my breasts in her hands and ran her lips between them, down my stomach. I touch her eyelids and her forehead and her hair and her fingers and the back of her neck. And she enters me and I am everywhere at once and nowhere at all. And I remember everything and find that nothing matters. And for a moment, for a moment or two that lasts forever, we become one person. And I forget, we forget, that we were ever alive. And everything makes perfect sense.

NOTES FOR THIS SPEECH:

'Dr. Kevorkian': doctor who championed the 'right to die' for patients;

'The Tropic of Cancer': book banned for its sexual nature.

You may like to change some words to bring the references up to date: **See Note 2.**

You start talking of death, and move to talking of love – a great change: **See Notes 4 and 5.**

You are talking to the audience: **See Note 6.**

From PTERODACTYLS by Nicky Silver, copyright © 1994 by Nicky Silver. Reprinted by permission The Gersh Agency on behalf of the Author.

16

TWILIGHT: LOS ANGELES, 1992

Anna Deavere Smith

FIRST PERFORMANCES	Los Angeles 1993; New York 1994
AWARDS	Nominated for the *Tony Award for Best Play*.
	Anna Deavere Smith nominated for the *Tony Award for Best Actress in a Play*.
CHARACTER	Josie
PLAYED BY	Anna Deavere Smith
CHARACTER'S AGE	20s
CHARACTER'S TYPE	The author performed all the different characters in this play as a one-woman show. This character is an uncalled witness to the George Holliday beating, at the Simi Valley trial.
TIME AND PLACE	1992; Los Angeles.
SITUATION	A woman tells what she saw, and what she did, to try to get justice for her neighbour who was assaulted by police officers.

Josie:

We lived in Apartment A6,

right next to A8,

which is where George Holliday lived.

And, um,

the next thing we know is, um,

ten or twelve officers made a circle around him

and they started to hit him.
I remember
that they just not only hit him with sticks,
they also kicked him,
and one guy,
one police officer, even pummeled his fist
into his face,
and they were kicking him.
And then we were like 'Oh my goodness,'
and I was just watching.
I felt like 'Oh my goodness'
'cause it was really like
he was in danger there,
it was such
an oppressive atmosphere.
I knew it was wrong –
whatever he did –
I knew it was wrong,
I just knew in my heart
this is wrong –
you know they can't do that.
And even my husband was petrified.
My husband said, 'Let's go inside.'
He was trying to get me to come inside
and away from the scene,
but I said 'No.'
I said 'We have to stay here
and watch
because this is wrong.'
And he was just petrified –
he grew up in another country where this is prevalent,
police abuse is prevalent in Mexico –
so we stayed and we watched the whole thing.
And
I was scheduled to testify
and I was kind of upset at the outcome,

because I had a lot to say
and during the trial I kept in touch with the
prosecutor,
Terry White,
and I was just very upset
and I, um,
I had received a subpoena
and I told him, 'When do you want me to go?'
He says, 'I'll call you later and I'll give you a time.'
And the time came and went and he never called me,
so I started calling him.
I said 'Well, are you going to call me or not?'
And he says, 'I can't really talk to you
and I don't think we're going to be using you because
it contradicts what Melanie Singer said.'
And I faxed him a letter
and I told him that those officers were going to be acquitted
and one by one I explained these things to him in this letter
and I told him, 'If you do not put witnesses,
if you don't put one resident and testify to say what they saw,'
And I told him in the letter
that those officers were going to be acquitted.
But I really believe that he was dead set
on that video
and that the video would tell all,
but, you see, the video doesn't show you where those officers went
and assaulted Rodney King at the beginning.
You see that?
And I was so upset. I told my co-worker, I said, 'I had a terrible dream
that those guys were acquitted.'
And she goes, 'Oh no, they're not gonna be acquitted.'
She goes, 'You, you,
you know, don't think like that.'
I said 'I wasn't thinking I had a dream!'
I said, 'Look at this,
they were,

they were acquitted.'
Yeah, I do have dreams
that come true,
but not as vivid as that one.
I just had this dream and in my heart felt . . .
and I saw the
men
and it was in the courtroom and I just
had it in my heart . . .
something is happening
and I heard they were acquitted,
because dreams are made of some kind of indelible substance.
And my co-worker said, 'You shouldn't think like this,'
and I said, 'I wasn't thinking
it was a dream.'
And that's all,
and it came to pass.

NOTES FOR THIS SPEECH:

If you speak this piece as it is written, and so take a tiny pause at the end of each line and nowhere else, it will give you a naturalistic delivery. The speech is laid out the way the author wrote it; you can shorten it to meet your needs: **See Note 2**.

The more you believe that perhaps you will get a good result, the more you can plunge into despair when you don't: **See Note 5**.

An Afro-American accent is needed to match the lines; it is not important that your skin colour does: **See Note 7**.

17

HOLD PLEASE

Annie Weisman

FIRST PERFORMANCES	Costa Mesa 2001; New York 2003
AWARDS	Jeanine Serralles nominated for the *Drama Desk Award for Outstanding Featured Actress in a Play*.
CHARACTER	Jessica
PLAYED BY	Jillian Bach; Jeanine Serralles
CHARACTER'S AGE	24
TYPE	Upwardly mobile Valley Girl.
TIME AND PLACE	The present; a modern office.
SITUATION	Diana, the new (female) boss has just started work, as Jessica operates the morning switchboard, after a disastrous night.

Jessica is alone at her desk, with a scarf tied elaborately around her neck, and a black eye.

Jessica: SolomonGreenspanSachs. No he's not d'you want his voicemail. No I don't. Nope. No. No. No, I'm sorry. Nope. Will do, thanks. SolomonGreenspan Sachs. Hi! A lot better, thanks. Well, it's not pulsing and painful anymore. Now it's starting to tingle. The doctor said that means it's going to heal. I can start putting makeup on it tomorrow he said. It looks like I won't even need antibiotics. *[Beat.]* What time? *[Beat.]* OK. Chinese at eight tonight. Whatever you say! *[A loud buzz.]* That was her! Our new boss! He's a she! It's a girl! Her name is Diana. She has this buzzing thing. *[Buzz.]* Yes, Diana? *[Beat.]* Yes, there's a refrigerator in the executive break room you're free to use. Or I can put it in the support staff mini-fridge for you if you like. That would be no problem as well. If you'd like, I can show you some menus from which we order. There's a great salad place, okay Thai, and for something fun and different: Persian. They make these skewers? And just as an FYI, Erika, my cubiclemate, keeps a large tin of Altoids in the top drawer of her desk and we're all welcome to use them. *[Beat.]* Um, Hello? *[Buzz.]* Yes, Diana? Yes, we have a labeling machine. I'd be happy to bring it right in. It's good that you get your labeling done right away. Did I see on the bio you handed me that you went to Pepperdine? Did you know a guy there by the name of Micah Goranson? Red hair, green eyes, psych major, always wore a pair of Stop Sign Red classic Converse? He went to my high school, so I was just wondering. Hello? *[Beat.]* Jonathan? I think I have to go. I'll see you tonight my love. *[Buzz.]* Yes, Diana? Oh, I'll be right in with it. And if you were wondering about my eye. My boyfriend hit me. Hello? Diana? Hello? SolomonGreenspanSachs can I assist you? She's here! No he's not d'you want his voicemail.

NOTES FOR THIS SPEECH:

'FYI': for your information;

'Altoids': breath freshening mints;

'Pepperdine': independent college in California.

You can make huge changes in the way you talk to the different people: **See Note 5**.

You can indicate the sort of telephone receiver you have, or use a real one: **See Note 9**.

You could also operate a small buzzer to give the right sound effect.

18

THE HERBAL BED

Peter Whelan

FIRST PERFORMANCES	Stratford-upon-Avon 1996; London 1997; New York 1998
AWARDS	Nominated for the *Laurence Olivier Award for Best New Play*.
CHARACTER	Susanna
PLAYED BY	Teresa Banham; Kate Duchêne [UK]; Laila Robins [US]
CHARACTER'S AGE	late 20s
CHARACTER'S TYPE	She is an Elizabethan housewife; the daughter of William Shakespeare, and married to John Hall the local doctor.
TIME AND PLACE	1613; Susanna's garden in Stratford-upon-Avon.
SITUATION	Rafe, a married man and family friend, is visiting Susanna Hall in her garden – the garden where she grows all the herbs for the cordials she makes and sells.

Susanna: I need you more than you realise. Just as I'm myself . . . and my husband's wife . . . so he is himself, as well as his wife's husband. Five years have made him more himself, less mine. I married a man for a month or two. For the rest, I married medicine. He seemed to have such stature . . . and still does. I respect him, absolutely . . . but in those years, except at the beginning, I don't think . . . I *know* . . . he's never, of himself, reached out and embraced me . . . never really kissed me, by which I mean in pure love. Sometimes we're in the company of a very loving couple . . . well, take the Palmers . . . or Hamnet Sadler and his wife who're my father's age . . . but still he'll touch her hand, or lips, or her ear . . . and she'll open up such a loving smile at him. Well, I've seen a husband and wife leave this house and hug and kiss before they've gone three yards . . . as though trying to lift some blight they felt when they'd been with us. And when I see that I think my God! What a wilderness I'm in!

Rafe: No. It's a good marriage . . . When you stepped out of Holy Trinity it was seen as the most brilliant marriage of the town . . . the doctor and the poet's daughter! Ask around. Ask them. There's not a person living here who won't say, 'this is a good marriage!'

Susanna: Oh it's good in other ways, yes. I'd partly married him out of a fascination for medicine . . . and that's grown in me more and more, as, you might say, to compensate. In place of love he's let me learn a little of his art. I made my cordials . . . my famous cordials . . . and spent a great deal of time varying the ingredients and noting the results. He knew he had to make some kind of exchange, you see, however unspoken. So it became understood I would use the dispensary when the apothecaries were away. I never troubled him with how much I learned . . . nor ever talked about it with others in case he was criticised. It's been a pact between us . . . never discussed or challenged. Knowledge was there for the picking, as long as I used a small basket and kept it out of sight. But, oh, I wanted that fruit! I picked more and more . . . and didn't mind who knew. I wanted to be Helena . . . she's a character of my father's . . . the daughter of a doctor who's died. She cures the king of France with a cure she's inherited. And, for me, she becomes the doctor . . .

Rafe: You see yourself in her?

Susanna: I do . . . and I don't. I'm drawn to her inner passion. Oh . . . that's another thing. She loves a man who everyone will say she shouldn't love . . .

NOTES FOR THIS SPEECH:

'Holy Trinity': church in Stratford-upon-Avon;

'apothecaries': prepared and sold drugs and medicines in those days.

You will need to act the other character's speeches: **See Note 1**.

The last line reveals your hidden emotion: **See Note 5**.

19

JITNEY

August Wilson

FIRST PERFORMANCES	New York 2000; London 2001
AWARDS	**Won** the *Laurence Olivier Award for Best New Play*; nominated for the *Drama Desk Award for Outstanding New Play*.
CHARACTER	Rena
PLAYED BY	Michole Briana White [US]; Linda Powell [UK]
CHARACTER'S AGE	20s
CHARACTER'S TYPE	She is Darnell's girlfriend, and already a young black mother.
TIME AND PLACE	1977; Pittsburgh gypsy cab depot.
SITUATION	Rena is reacting to the news that her partner Darnell Youngblood, a Vietnam veteran, has bought a house without consulting her, or thinking of their daughter Jesse.

Rena: Darnell, you ain't bought no house without me. How many times in your life do you get to pick out a house?

Youngblood: Wait till you see it. It's real nice. It's all on one floor . . . it's got a basement . . . like a little den. We can put the TV down there. I told myself Rena's gonna like this. Wait till she see I bought her a house.

Rena: Naw, you bought a den for Darnell . . . that's what you did. So you can sit down there and watch your football games. But what about the kitchen? The bathroom? How many windows does it have in the bedroom? Is there some place for Jesse to play? How much closet space does it have? You can't just surprise me with a house and I'm supposed to say, 'Oh, Darnell, that's nice.' At one time I would have. But I'm not seventeen no more. I have responsibilities. I want to know if it has a hookup for a washer and dryer cause I got to wash Jesse's clothes. I want to know if it has a yard and do it have a fence and how far Jesse has to go to school. I ain't thinking about where to put the TV. That's not what's important to me. And you supposed to know, Darnell. You supposed to know what's important to me like I'm supposed to know what's important to you. I'm not asking you to do it by yourself. I'm here with you. We in this together. See . . . house or no house we still ain't got the food money. But if you had come and told me . . . if you had shared that with me . . . we could have went to my mother and we could have got eighty dollars for the house and still had money for food. You just did it all wrong, Darnell. I mean, you did the right thing but you did it wrong.

NOTES FOR THIS SPEECH:

A one act version of this play premiered in Pittsburgh in 1982.

'gypsy cab': taxicab that is licensed only to respond to calls but often cruises the streets for passengers.

You will need to act the other person's lines: **See Note 1**.

Make sure you don't play it all on one note: **See Notes 4 and 5**.

An Afro-American accent is needed to match the lines; it is not important that your skin colour does. **See Note 7**.

30s

20

SCENES FROM A MARRIAGE

Ingmar Bergman, translated by
Frederick J. Marker

FIRST PERFORMANCES	Munich 1981; London 1990
AWARDS	Penny Downie nominated for the *Laurence Olivier Award for Actress of the Year*.
CHARACTER	Marianne
PLAYED BY	Gaby Dohm [Germany]; Penny Downie [UK]
CHARACTER'S AGE	30s
CHARACTER'S TYPE	She is irresolute and dreamy.
TIME AND PLACE	Present; the couple's flat, anywhere.
SITUATION	Johan, her husband, has just told her he is leaving her for a younger woman.

Marianne: So long.

Johan: I may be home in a week.

Marianne: If only you were. We'd make a fresh start in every way. We'd get rid of all the routine and the slack habits. We'd talk over the past. We'd try to find where we've gone wrong. You'd never hear any accusations. I promise you. It's all so unreal. I don't know what to do about it. You're shutting me out. Can't you promise to come back? Then I'd know *something*. I mean, you can't just leave me without any hope. It's not fair. Even if you have no intention of returning, you could at least *say* you're coming home again.

Johan: I must go now, Marianne.

Marianne: *[She tries to hold onto him, but he tears himself free and leaves. She stands for a long time, then goes to the telephone and dials a number.]* Hello,

Fredrik, it's Marianne. Sorry to wake you. Is Birgit there? No, it doesn't matter. Let her sleep. How are things? Oh, you like puttering around alone at this hour. No, I won't keep you long. No, it's cloudy here. Oh, how nice for you. Well, I wanted to talk to you about something. No, I just wanted someone to talk to. You and Birgit *are* our friends. I must have . . . I must . . . it's all so unreal, Fredrik. You see – *[Pause.]* – I'm about to burst into tears any moment and I don't *want* to cry. You see, Johan has fallen in love with another woman. Her name's Paula, and they're going off to Paris today. Can't you talk to Johan and ask him to wait a bit? He needn't rush off headlong like that. What? You've already talked to him? Oh, I see. I see. So you and Birgit have known all along. You've known the whole time and not said a word to me? What the hell kind of friends are you anyway? How could you be so goddamn rotten and unfair to me? I don't care what you say. And all the times we've met and talked and you have known and never said anything. *[In a fury.]* Nice friends you are! You can go to hell with your explanations. Just how many people have known of this? Oh, quite a number. I'm glad to know. *[She flings the phone down. She bites her hand to stop herself from screaming.]*

NOTES FOR THIS SPEECH:

We need to understand what your husband is saying to you: **See Note 1.**

You can change the names of the people if it suits your purposes better: **See Note 3.**

The more you play that you think your friends know nothing of your plight, the greater will be the contrast in your attitude when you discover they already knew, and then again when *everyone* seems to have known: **See Note 5.**

You can act out trying to stop him leaving: **See Note 8.**

21

JOINED AT THE HEAD

Catherine Butterfield

FIRST PERFORMANCES	New York 1992
AWARDS	Nominated for the *Drama Desk Award for Outstanding New Play*.
CHARACTER	Maggie
PLAYED BY	Ellen Parker
CHARACTER'S AGE	late 30s
CHARACTER'S TYPE	She is tough, even unlikeable; a woman without friends who is learning how to become one.
TIME AND PLACE	Now; Boston.
SITUATION	Maggie is on a promotional tour for her new novel.

Maggie: I was walking down Newbury Street in Boston on a very brisk, very clear day, late afternoon. Low on the horizon, the white winter sun shone directly in my face. It dazzled me, this light. I could see shadow forms of people coming toward me, but I couldn't make out faces, and I couldn't make out buildings, and I felt like I was almost blind, although my eyes were wide open. How to describe it – I felt like a camera with its lens open too far. And you know, it's funny about the drivers in Boston, they don't honk very much. They drive like madmen, but they don't honk. Which is unexpected to a New Yorker, who expects not only honking but yelling, sirens, distant gunfire. So here I was, having this strange, silent walk down Newbury Street, strange not only because it seemed so civilized, but because, being blinded by this light, my sense of hearing was unusually keen. And without meaning to, I found myself eavesdropping on a number of conversations.

[We hear other people's conversations.]

Maggie: That was it, really. Conversations. Fragments of conversations. Who knows where they were meant to lead? But I became so aware of how much life is going on all the time, how many stories, how many people are out there with their absolute reality that has nothing to do with my absolute reality. To them, I'm the backdrop. To me, they're mine. How often do we think of ourselves as backdrops for other peoples' lives? Not too often, I guess. We prefer to think of ourselves as being terribly significant. I remember being in New York once when a piece of scaffolding fell and bisected the head of a person a half a block ahead of me. I arrived in time to see the carnage, the hysteria. And I started thinking about the guy who'd been killed. An actor in his thirties, I read a few days later. The center of his own particular universe, until his universe was suddenly snatched away from him. All the rest of us, on that New York afternoon on 57th Street, were the backdrop for the particular drama that was his life. How strange it would have been for him to know ahead of time that the supporting cast was going to play the show out without him. A play with a vacuum where the leading man is supposed to be? Impossible! We all live with that illusion, don't we? And we all parade the streets daily, back and forth, oblivious to the fact that the next piece of scaffolding may be meant for us. And convinced that really, deep down in the truest part of life, we are nobody's backdrop.

NOTES FOR THIS SPEECH:

Let the different events affect you, so you go on a journey of changing emotions: **See Note 4.**

Between the two parts of your speech is where the audience hears snatches of people talking. This is a good opportunity for you to act different versions of listening. **See Note 5.**

You are talking to the audience: **See Note 6.**

22

STEAMING

Nell Dunn

FIRST PERFORMANCES	London 1981; New York 1982
AWARDS	Nominated for the *Laurence Olivier Award for Best Comedy of the Year*.
	Georgina Hale nominated for the *Laurence Olivier Award for Best Comedy Performance of the Year*.
	Judith Ivey **won** the *Tony Award for Best Actress in a Featured Role in a Play*, **and** the *Drama Desk Award for Outstanding Featured Actress in a Play*.
CHARACTER	Josie
PLAYED BY	Georgina Hale [UK]; Judith Ivey [US]
CHARACTER'S AGE	about 34
CHARACTER'S TYPE	She is a working-class woman, unashamed in talking of her life and troubles.
TIME AND PLACE	Now; a Turkish Bath in London.
SITUATION	The Baths are where the local women can let their hair down, safe from the men in their lives, and Josie has just arrived to meet the others, including her friends Nancy and Violet.

Josie: Look at my face! *[She takes off the glasses and reveals a bruised face.]* He done that last night. He'd been drinking. He put his hands round my throat and said, 'I'm going to kill you.' 'You're touched', I said. 'I'm going to gas you,' he says in a horrible deep voice. 'Don't be silly,' I says, 'Let me go.' But inside I was really scared. 'Get on the bed,' he says. 'No,' I says. 'I'm not going to have nothing to do with you,' So wallop, he hits me – I don't know what happened next! . . . It all started because I was wearing a new dress. 'Now you've got your job you think you're the only woman in the world! Ha! Ha!' he goes. 'I suppose you think you're a beauty queen? Ha!' My poor ear, how come I always get hit on me left side?

Nancy: Why on earth did you take him back?

Josie: 'Don't throw dirty water away till you've got clean,' my Mum always says. *[Pause. Then angrily.]* How am I going to pay my bills? It's all very well for women like you, you can afford to live without men – I can't! At fifteen I was going early morning cleaning with my Mum! At sixteen I was having a baby . . . You were still at school. *[Pause.]* I'm sick of poverty. Guess what time I worked till? From Saturday night I worked till seven o'clock Sunday morning on the boats, barmaiding – seven o'clock in the morning and I earned £30.

Nancy: That's wonderful.

Josie: It wasn't wonderful – it was bloody hard work but at least I got my rates money. When I got home I sat down in a chair and fell fast asleep. That was Sunday and now what do you think came through me door this morning? Another fucking bill – this time for me television. I don't see why they keep sending me all these bills – it does me nerves up trying to pay them when I'm on me own . . . He hasn't been near or by for a week. *[Pause.]*

Well, Sunday afternoon I was so tired I wore these old jeans and socks and guess what? *He* turns up! *[Imitating JERRY:]* 'You look disgusting, you have let yerself go. No-one will ever look at you if you dress like that.' Oh, I was choked! I was so choked, I thought is it really worth it, my struggle to stand on me own feet? *[To VIOLET.]* So I took him back. 'One day I'm going to kill you,' he says. Then we has it, but it didn't do me no good so after he'd gone I got me Pifco out. I had to. I had so much tension in me it was like a screw going round – the back of my neck. 'Books,' he says, 'Read books.' 'I can't read books, they bore me. Books, books, books, I'll look like a book one of these days – I want a bit of life not books.' I want to be somebody, to have done something. At the moment all I'm going to get on my gravestone is: 'She was a good fuck!' I don't want to be remembered just for that.

NOTES FOR THIS SPEECH:

'barmaiding': working in a bar;

'rates money': money for the local property tax;

'Pifco': battery operated device.

Make sure the sense of the other character's lines is acted: **See Note 1**.

If the speech is too long for your purposes, you could cut the third paragraph beginning 'It wasn't wonderful' and trim the bit about books: **See Note 2**.

Feel free to change words: **See Note 3**.

Be happy when you say 'Then we has it' in order to change gear when it all goes wrong. On the last line, try choosing the word 'just'. It's unexpected, and gives an interesting extra dimension to your character: **See Note 5**.

It should be in a cockney accent, but only if done well: **See Note 7**.

23

SARAH, SARAH

Daniel Goldfarb

FIRST PERFORMANCES	New York 2004
AWARDS	J. Smith-Cameron nominated for the *Drama Desk Award for Outstanding Actress in a Play*.
CHARACTER	Jeannie
PLAYED BY	J. Smith-Cameron
CHARACTER'S AGE	39
CHARACTER'S TYPE	She is an unmarried child psychologist.
TIME AND PLACE	2001; a Holiday Inn room in China.
SITUATION	She and her father Arthur are in China for her to adopt an orphaned child.

ARTHUR is taking a shower. JEANNIE enters from her room. She takes the cell phone from her father's bag. She dials, waits, impatient.

Jeannie: Hi, Ma. No, I'm sorry we didn't call yesterday, it was just so crazy. Dad's in the shower. And I just, I wanted to – *[Falling apart.]* Oh Ma.

I think there's something wrong with the baby. I don't know. She's just kind of limp. She has these sort of scary dead eyes, like she's permanently cross-eyed. I didn't recognize her from the picture they sent. She's *not* chubby, they stuffed her clothes in that picture to make her look healthy. She's weak. You can see it. She's the smallest one in the group.

She – uhh, she has this big funny-shaped head. It's all I could see for the first – her forehead kind of juts out, and the back of her head is flat, you know from lying down in the crib, I guess, not being held enough – And her body is so tiny. Dad says she looks like Tweety Bird.

Fourteen pounds – ten months. Ten and a half – No the birthday is real, I asked that too. She's just malnourished. She has almost no hair. And she has this rash, I don't think they kept them very clean. Oh, Ma. Please don't tell Dad I called you. Promise me. He's acting so weird. He won't even hold her.

She's asleep now. The group is all going to the orphanage in about an hour. I really wanna go, but I think we have to take her to the hospital instead. She had a fever when we got her, and when I took her temperature this morning, it's gotten worse, 102, I know, but I made a list of questions, you know, to ask whoever took care of her there. Maybe they know something. Maybe they know something to just get her to snap out of this. I was hoping after a good night's sleep she'd snap out of it. It's like she's in a trance, ma. No, he won't go for me. I don't know. He says he doesn't want to leave me alone. It's bullshit. I guess I could. That's a good idea – There's a young couple. Miles and . . . Maggie, I think. Maybe they could. *[The shower goes off.]* Oh God. He's done. Promise you won't say anything. Whatever it is, it is. But, I just hope she's OK.

I love you too. *[The bathroom door opens. JEANNIE wipes her face, puts on a brave face.]*

Arthur: Is that Mommy?

Jeannie: Yeah. You wanna speak to her?

NOTES FOR THIS SPEECH:

'Tweety Bird': cartoon character with an enormous head.

It will be easy to act Arthur's line: See Note 1.

It would be fatal to play it all on one level; find the varieties: See Note 4.

Make sure that Arthur and the bathroom are downstage of you, so we can see you turn from the phone to see if he is coming in during the speech, and also see the change in your face when he enters. The baby could be in a crib by your side, preferably not the same side as the bathroom. This gives you differing eyelines: See Note 8.

It would be useful to have a telephone handset: See Note 9.

24

SNAKEBIT

David Marshall Grant

FIRST PERFORMANCES	Chicago 1993; New York 1999
AWARDS	Nominated for the *Drama Desk Award for Outstanding Play*.
CHARACTER	Jenifer
PLAYED BY	Talia Balsam; Jodie Markell
CHARACTER'S AGE	30s
CHARACTER'S TYPE	She is an ex-actress, now the mother of a sick child.
TIME AND PLACE	August; the living room of a Spanish-style house in Los Angeles.
SITUATION	Jenifer and Jonathan are visiting their friend Michael in LA, as Jonathan is up for a very important role. Jenifer once had an affair with Michael, although he is gay, and alone with him, she tells of why she gave up acting.

Jenifer: I don't want to be an actress. I hate acting. I've always hated acting. It fills me with nothing but self-loathing. There, I said it. And you know, you do your affirmations, you know, your prayers that you'll be like, you know, so filled with self-love, that all that won't matter. What am I saying? The whole thing's a joke. You know why I don't want to act? And don't tell Jonathan this, I've never told anybody this. I started to stutter. On stage. Can you believe that? Honestly I would get to a word in the script, and when I came to it, I wouldn't be able to say it. I would freeze. Every time I would get to it. I couldn't get it out.

Michael: You started to stutter?

Jenifer: I get fixated on a word. Last time, I was playing the blind Mexican flower vendor in *Streetcar Named Desire*. Don't ask me why. And all I had to do was say, *'Flores para los muertos.'* There, I said it now. *'Flores para los muertos.'* I had nothing else to say, just that. I sat around waiting all night. *'Flores para los muertos.' 'Flores para los muertos.'* I couldn't say it. Now I can say it. It's pathetic.

Michael: What couldn't you say?

Jenifer: *Muertos.* I couldn't say, *Muertos.* It wouldn't come out. I ended up saying, *'Flores para los* dead people.' Blanche DuBois accused me of sabotaging her performance.

Michael: Well, fuck her. You adapted under difficult circumstances. What did she want you to do? Not say anything?

Jenifer: She wanted me to say the line right. That's what I was not getting paid to do. And Jonathan made me feel so . . . You know, why don't I just leave him? I really should just leave him. *[Beat.]* Michael?

NOTES FOR THIS SPEECH:

'Flores para los muertos': flowers for the dead; the flowers put on graves.

You will need to let us know what Michael says to you: **See Note 1**.

You might want to soften the language a little: **See Note 3**.

Your very first line should be a shock, and the last line a surprise: **See Note 5**.

25

PERFECT DAYS

Liz Lochhead

FIRST PERFORMANCES	Edinburgh 1998; London 1999
AWARDS	Nominated for the *Laurence Olivier Award for Best New Play*.
CHARACTER	Barbs
PLAYED BY	Siobhan Redmond
CHARACTER'S AGE	late 30s
CHARACTER'S TYPE	She is expensively dressed, and very flamboyantly attractive.
TIME AND PLACE	Now; a very large apartment in Glasgow, Scotland.
SITUATION	Barbs has come round to Alice's flat to give her an expensive haircut. She is a celebrity hairdresser – starting to get drowned by the sound of her own biological clock.

Barbs: So, Alice, I was telling you, we get to Glasgow airport, guy on the desk recognises me, we get an upgrade, very nice, thank you very much, First Class practically empty, great, spread out a bit, relax, the champagne cocktails, the blue blue sky, the white fluffy clouds beneath us . . . I'm feeling: OK maybe he's not got the highest IQ in the world but he does have a gorgeous profile and at least he's not wearing that fucking awful jumper that he turned up in wan night, tucked into his trousers can you believe, and gave me a red neck in front of Brendan from work.

I mean true and everlasting love it is not, but he's a nice guy and all that, own teeth, daft about me, well so far, it's only been three or four weeks, defin-ately dead keen, or so I've been led to believe by the dinners, the phonecalls, the nipping my heid about Paris – how he used to live there, how there are all like to take me, so there we are, we get to the hotel and here they've overbooked so this time we get an automatic upgrade to the four star no problem, it's gorgeous, the corner room, the fruitbowl, the flowers, the complimentary chocolates, the half bottle of champagne, the big kingsize bed all turned down at the corner . . . And – now, to let you know, Alice – back home in Glasgow I've been avoiding it, by the way, because truth to tell I do not really fancy him, at least I do not fancy him when I am actually *with* him, I've been, frankly, postponing the inevitable for this weekend where I have calculated, quite correctly according to my Predictor Kit, I will be *ovulating* – and he says to me he can't sleep with me because he's Met Someone and he's fallen in love! No, correction, he can *sleep* with me, but we can't have sex because that would be him being unfaithful to his new wee dolly inamorata.

I'm like: What? I'm like: What are we doing here? And Why? He's like: well, it's a fantastic city, and I'm his best friend – best friend! – and he wants to show me it and he didn't want to disappoint me!

Chin*ese*!

Alice: Martians . . . *[Meaning men in general.]*

Barbs: I'm like . . . naah, he won't be able to last out, *but* we go for dinner, we walk along the Seine in the moonlight, we have a couple of brandies, and yet, no, quite oblivious to me and all my brand new extortionate La Perla flimsies bought special, nope – bedtime, he pecks me chastely on the cheek and falls fast and instantly asleep, snoring away like billyo while I am lying there wide awake and just bloody raging.

Because, apart from the galling fact that one of my dwindling supply of eggs is up there, yet again going to waste for want of the Sparky Sperm the Tadpole with its name on it, now that I can't have him do I not start to fancy him something chronic? Torture.

NOTES FOR THIS SPEECH:

'wan': one;

'heid': head;

'wee': small;

'inamorata': female sweetheart;

'La Perla': a brand of glamorous underwear;

'Chinese': indication of something completely unlike herself, like Martians.

You may like to change some words, if the originals do not work for your situation: **See Note 3**.

The non-standard spelling reflects the Scottish accent: **See Note 7**.

You are doing her hair, so she can be downstage of you, and you can either have a real comb or scissors in your hand; or mime the whole range of equipment: **See Notes 8 and 9**.

26

SIN (A CARDINAL DEPOSED)

Michael Murphy

FIRST PERFORMANCES	New York 2004
AWARDS	Nominated for the *Drama Desk Award for Outstanding Play*.
CHARACTER	Maryetta Dussourd
PLAYED BY	Cynthia Darlow
CHARACTER'S AGE	30s
CHARACTER'S TYPE	She is the mother of a victim of priest abuse, a devout Catholic.
TIME AND PLACE	2002; Boston Court Room.
SITUATION	A mother is testifying in the case against Cardinal Law, that he knowingly allowed paedophile priests, such as Father Geoghan, to continue their abuse of children.

Maryetta Dussourd: Um, Father Geoghan invited himself to our home so he could get to know the family. Which – any priest that's child orientated. He was CYO, he had the altar boys he was in charge of. That seems perfectly natural. He's around children all the time. So he came and he dropped down to meet the family. And it just became he'd drop in when he wanted to drop in. He'd talk to me about the prayer group, um, and things like that, how he could be a help with the children. So he seemed like he was a friend. Um. The way that I found out was that my sister made a phone call to me and she had told me that my sons had been raped by Father John Geoghan. And that I needed to speak to my sons. And that's how I found out. And immediately after, I took the older child and I separated him and I talked with him. And . . . My child became filled with fear. He was crying and shaking. He told me that Father John Geoghan said that I wouldn't believe him. That I . . . had too much faith in the church . . . and that I wouldn't believe him. And then my son told me how things happened. He told me how Father Geoghan threatened him. And immediately my child tried to run out our back door – and I, I pulled my son back and I told my son that I would never, ever stop loving him. And I told my son that no way could Father Geoghan ever separate us. Well, the thing is, it separated us, it separated everybody in that . . . I felt so guilty. I would dress my little four year old and my little six year and nine year old and feed them, and thinking I was loving them so much and they would just look at you with the littlest, sweetest faces. And I caused their violation. If I hadn't invited that man into my house . . . I'm the reason all of this has happened to everybody. I'm the guilty person. Um . . . And I had to take care of it. And I did that. And I knew the vicar of this area and I went to that person. And he was overwhelmed. Because it was the first time he had ever heard of it. And he invited Father John Geoghan down to his house, to the rectory, had lunch with him. They sat across the table from each other, and when he asked Father John Geoghan – Father John Geoghan readily admitted it. And he said to the vicar, oh, well, it was only two families.

NOTES FOR THIS SPEECH:

'CYO': Catholic Youth Organization.

Use the three 'Um's' as moments when you are working out what to say next.

This speech starts off sweetly, and builds to an emotional climax: **See Note 4**.

Make sure the last comment from the priest comes as a complete surprise: **See Note 5**.

You are giving evidence, but could well talk to the audience: **See Note 6**.

From SIN (A CARDINAL DEPOSED) by Michael Murphy, copyright © 2006 by New York University and the Massachusetts Institute of Technology. Used by permission of TDR/The Drama Review.

27

'NIGHT MOTHER: A PLAY

Marsha Norman

FIRST PERFORMANCES	New York 1983; London 2006
AWARDS	Won *The Pulitzer Prize for Drama*; nominated for the *Tony Award for Best Play*.
	Kathy Bates nominated for the *Tony Award for Best Actress in a Play*.
	Anne Pitoniak [US: Mama] nominated for the *Tony Award for Best Actress in a Play*.
CHARACTER	Jessie
PLAYED BY	Kathy Bates [US]; Fiona Douglas [UK]
CHARACTER'S AGE	late 30s to early 40s
CHARACTER'S TYPE	She has a peaceful energy, but is intent on suicide.
TIME AND PLACE	Now; living room of a small house on an isolated road in America.
SITUATION	She shares the house with her mother, her marriage ended in divorce, her absent son is a good-for-nothing, and she is preparing for her suicide in the strong belief that this is the best thing for her to do, and is telling her mother so.

Jessie: No, Mama! We wouldn't have more talks like tonight, because it's this next part that's made this last part so good, Mama. No, Mama. *This* is how I have my say. This is how I say what I thought about it *all* and I say No. To Dawson and Loretta and the Red Chinese and epilepsy and Ricky and Cecil and you. And me. And hope. I say No! *[Then going to MAMA on the sofa.]* Just let me go easy, Mama.

Mama: How can I let you go?

Jessie: You can because you have to. It's what you've always done.

Mama: You are my child!

Jessie: I am what became of your child. *[MAMA cannot answer.]* I found an old baby picture of me. And it was somebody else, not me. It was somebody pink and fat who never heard of sick or lonely, somebody who cried and got fed, and reached up and got held and kicked but didn't hurt anybody, and slept whenever she wanted to, just by closing her eyes. Somebody who mainly just laid there and laughed at the colors waving around over her head and chewed on a polka-dot whale and woke up knowing some new trick nearly every day and rolled over and drooled on the sheet and felt your hand pulling my quilt back up over me. That's who I started out and this is who is left. *[There is no self-pity here.]* That's what this is about. It's somebody I lost, all right, it's my own self. Who I never was. Or who I tried to be and never got there. Somebody I waited for who never came. And never will. So, see, it doesn't much matter what else happens in the world or in this house, even. I'm what was worth waiting for and I didn't make it. Me . . . who might have made a difference to me . . . I'm not going to show up, so there's no reason to stay, except to keep you company, and that's . . . not reason enough because I'm not . . . very good company. *[A pause.]* Am I.

NOTES FOR THIS SPEECH:

You will need to act your mother's lines: **See Note 1.**

Find the happiness in the baby moments, to give you the biggest contrast with your present feelings: **See Notes 4 and 5.**

28

LOST IN YONKERS

Neil Simon

FIRST PERFORMANCES	Washington 1991; New York 1991; London 1992
AWARDS	Won *The Pulitzer Prize for Drama*, and the *Tony Award for Best Play*, and the *Drama Desk Award for Outstanding New Play*; nominated for the *Laurence Olivier Award for Best Comedy*.
	Mercedes Ruehl won the *Tony Award for Best Actress in a Play*, and the *Drama Desk Award for Outstanding Actress in a Play*.
	Irene Worth [US: Grandma] won the *Tony Award for Best Actress in a Featured Role in a Play* and the *Drama Desk Award for Outstanding Featured Actress in a Play*.
	Kevin Spacey [US: Louie] won the *Tony Award for Best Actor in a Featured Role in a Play* and the *Drama Desk Award for Outstanding Featured Actor*.
	Rosemary Harris [UK: Grandma] nominated for the *Laurence Olivier Award for Best Actress in a Supporting Role*.
CHARACTER	Bella
PLAYED BY	Mercedes Ruehl [US]; Maureen Lipman [UK]
CHARACTER'S AGE	mid-30s
CHARACTER'S TYPE	She is pathetically affectionate; and a mess at dressing.
TIME AND PLACE	1942; an apartment in Yonkers, New York.

Bella: Me! He wants *me!* He wants to marry me! *[She starts to cry.]* I want to
marry *him* . . . I want to have his children . . . I want my own babies.
Louie: Jesus Christ!
Grandma: Dot's enough! . . . I don't vant to hear dis anymore!
Bella: You think I can't have healthy babies, Momma? Well, I can . . . I'm as
strong as an ox. I've worked in that store and taken care of you by myself since
I'm twelve years old, that's how strong I am . . . Like *steel*, Momma. Isn't that how
we're supposed to be? . . . But my babies won't die because I'll love them and take
care of them . . . And they won't get sick like me or Gert or be weak like Eddie and
Louie . . . My babies will be happier than we were because I'll teach them to be
happy . . . Not to grow up and run away or never visit when they're older and not
be able to breathe because they're so frightened . . . and never, *ever* to make
them spend their lives rubbing my back and my legs because you never had
anyone around who loved you enough to want to touch you because you made
it so clear you never wanted to be touched with love . . . Do you know what it's
like to touch steel, Momma? It's hard and it's cold and I want to be warm and soft
with my children . . . Let me have my babies, Momma. Because I have to love
somebody. I have to love someone who'll love me back before I die . . . Give me
that, Momma, and I promise you, you'll never worry about being alone . . .
Because you'll have us . . . Me and my husband and my babies . . . Louie, tell
her how wonderful that would be . . . Gert, wouldn't that make her happy? . . .
Momma? . . . Please say yes . . . I need you to say yes . . . Please? *[Her mother
leaves the room.]*

Hold me . . . Somebody please hold me.

We can imagine what the others are saying to you: **See Note 1.**

You get more and more desperate as you do not get approval from your mother, despite what you say: **See Note 4.**

Place the others downstage of you, so we see your face as you plead with them; and make sure the audience know that your mother has left the stage: **See Note 8.**

29

THE MEMORY OF WATER

Shelagh Stephenson

FIRST PERFORMANCES	London 1996; New York 1998
AWARDS	Won the *Laurence Olivier Award for Best New Comedy.*
CHARACTER	Catherine
PLAYED BY	Matilda Zeigler, Julia Sawalha [UK]; Seana Kofoed [US]
CHARACTER'S AGE	33
CHARACTER'S TYPE	She is a girl about town, who passions are shopping, doomed love affairs, and drugs.
TIME AND PLACE	Now; a suburban house in England.
SITUATION	Three sisters have met up for their mother's funeral. Catherine is the youngest, the most insecure, and is sharing her memories and worries with her sisters.

Catherine: Fuck it. *[Silence. She bursts into racking sobs.]*

I went to this counsellor – did I tell you this? – or a therapist or something and she said I had this problem and the problem was, I give too much, I just do too much for other people, I'm just a very giving person, and I never get any credit for any of it. I haven't even got any friends. I mean, I have but I don't like most of them, especially the women, and I try really hard, it's just I'm very sensitive and I get taken for a ride, nothing ever goes right, every time, I mean, every time it's the same – like with men. What is it with men? I mean, I don't have a problem with men or anything. I love men. I've been to bed with seventy-eight of them, I counted, so obviously there's not a problem or anything, it's just he didn't even apologize or anything and how can he say on the phone he doesn't want to see me any more? I mean, why now? Why couldn't he have waited? I don't know what to do, why does it always go wrong? I don't want to be on my own, I'm sick of people saying I'll be better off on my own, I'm not that sort of person, I can't do it. I did everything for him, I was patient and all the things you're supposed to be and people kept saying don't accept this from him, don't accept that, like, you know, when he stayed out all night, not very often, I mean once or twice, and everyone said tell him to fuck off, but how could I because what if he did? Because they all do, everyone I've ever met does, they all disappear and I don't know if it's me or what. I don't want to be on my own, I can't stand it, I know it's supposed to be great but I don't think it is. I can't help it, it's no good pretending, it's fucking lonely and I can't bear it. *[She rushes out of the room.]*

NOTES FOR THIS SPEECH:

You can always use the alternative word 'sod' for language that may be inappropriate for your situation: **See Note 3**.

You should start low, in order to build to your explosive exit: **See Note 4**.

Because there are two other characters on stage with you, and there are a number of question marks in the speech, they would probably want to interrupt you with words of comfort. The trick is for you to come in quickly with each new thought. Place your sisters so you can swivel from one to the other: **See Note 8**.

30

HAPGOOD

Tom Stoppard

FIRST PERFORMANCES	London 1988; New York 1994
AWARDS	Stockard Channing nominated for the *Drama Desk Award for Outstanding Actress in a Play*.
CHARACTER	Hapgood
PLAYED BY	Felicity Kendal [UK]; Stockard Channing [US]
CHARACTER'S AGE	35
CHARACTER'S TYPE	She is head of Britain's secret service, also known as Betty.
TIME AND PLACE	1980s; photographer's studio in Cold War London.
SITUATION	Someone is leaking secrets to the Russians, and Ridley is investigating. Hapgood poses as her own twin sister Celia, working as a fashion photographer; nothing is what it seems.

Hapgood: *[She opens the door to a stranger, RIDLEY. Casually.]* Oh, shit.

Ridley: I'm Ernest.

Hapgood: Well, you're not what I want, so keep your clothes on. Stupid bugger! Not you, darling, come in anyway. *[She is already heading for the telephone.]* What did they do? Pick you from the catalogue? I'll try and sort it out – charge them for half a day if it looks like their fault – it won't be the first time – *[Now into the phone.]* It's Celia, I want Fred. Would you mind not wandering around.

[Into the phone.] Hello, darling, you're losing your grip – I said a Roman soldier, not an Italian waiter, and also he looks queer to me . . . Don't tell me what I mean, you're gay, he's queer, he's got a queer look about him. He won't

sell bamboo shoots to a fucking panda, never mind boxer shorts . . . Well, I'll look at his body and let you know – Fred? – Have you gone? – No, the phone clicked – *[She looks around and finds that the room is empty.]* Hey –? What's his name? *[She calls out.]* Victor!

Ridley: Hang up.

Hapgood: What do you think you're doing? *[Into phone.]* Is he a regular? . . . Well, I don't fancy him – *[That's as far as the phone call gets because RIDLEY, still maintaining a sort of thoughtful cruise, disconnects the call.]*

Now, listen – *[He looks at her. She goes from fear to relief.]* You're Betty's friend. Bloody hell, you gave me a turn. I thought, this isn't Victor, this is a nutter, it's the Kensington strangler, God, I am sorry, darling, I'm Celia, don't be offended, being rude about the models is the house style, it saves a lot of nonsense about being paid for the reshoot if it needs one, and anyway you do look like an Italian waiter. What does Betty want? – I don't owe her any favours, she never does me any, I mean there must be lots of photographic work going in the spy racket. She says I won't keep my mouth shut – I'm going to blab that I'm working for MI5 to everybody I meet? – Is it five or six? – Can you smell burning? – Oh, sod! *[She leaves the room in a hurry.]*

NOTES FOR THIS SPEECH:

'MI5': Britain's equivalent of the CIA.

The language might be too strong for your purposes: **See Note 3.**

Make sure you are very different when pretending to work as a photographer, to being the pretend sister to the head of MI5: **See Note 5.**

On the phone, you also call out remarks to the strange visitor, as you keep getting his name wrong. Make sure we know where he is: **See Note 8.**

This piece gives you plenty of opportunity to move about and do different bits of business: **See Note 9.**

31

THE MINEOLA TWINS

Paula Vogel

FIRST PERFORMANCES	Juneau 1996; New York 1999
AWARDS	Swoosie Kurtz nominated for the *Drama Desk Award for Outstanding Actress in a Play*.
CHARACTER	Myrna
PLAYED BY	Luan Schooler; Swoosie Kurtz
CHARACTER'S AGE	30s
CHARACTER'S TYPE	She is the good twin Myrna to her evil twin Myra. They are always on the opposite sides of the American experience.
TIME AND PLACE	1960s Nixon administration; a bank in downtown Mineola.
SITUATION	The good twin is getting her son Kenny psyched up ready to commit a white collar crime that will rid them of the evil twin.

Myrna: You know the story of the prodigal son? This man had two sons, right, and one worked hard in the fields from dawn to dusk. He never gave his parents cause to worry. The other son was a real *fuck-up*. I'm sorry, no other word will do. He never saved one thin dime, and he drank whatever money he filched from the family business. The prodigal son got into trouble with the law. He had to hide in this foreign land far across the borders, and a price was on his head. And he thought – Wait a minute, I'll bet I can get Mom sorry for me, and she'll dip into the old man's pockets when he's asleep. And so he came dragging home in clothes that hadn't been washed in weeks. And his aged parents bailed him out.

They drew his bathwater. They washed his clothes. And they barbecued up filet mignon. And do you know what the good son felt, when he came home from the fields and saw his evil brother getting the ticker-tape parade? *What am I, ground chuck?*

Ken: Mom? Mom?

Myrna: The Good Brother bided his time, and then went to the cops in the other country and turned his sorry brother in; took the reward, and invested it. And then, in a hostile takeover, he got control of his father's business. He sent his parents to a nice, clean nursing home where they had arts therapy. And when the prodigal son was finally released from the hoosegow, he had to beg in the marketplace, until the Prodigal Son finally *died*. And the Good Son danced and danced. Happy Ending!

NOTES FOR THIS SPEECH:

'filet mignon': best and most expensive steak cut;

'ground chuck': ground up meat, the cheapest option;

'hoosegow': slang for a jail.

It is easy to act the interruption: **See Note 1.**

You may need to change the language a little: **See Note 3.**

Find all the humour you can in this modern variation of a bible story: **See Note 5.**

32

THREE BIRDS ALIGHTING ON A FIELD

Timberlake Wertenbaker

FIRST PERFORMANCES	London 1988; New York 1994
AWARDS	Nominated for the *Laurence Olivier Award for Best New Play*.
	Harriet Walter nominated for the *Drama Desk Award for Outstanding Actress in a Play*.
CHARACTER	Biddy
PLAYED BY	Harriet Walter [UK and US]
CHARACTER'S AGE	30s
CHARACTER'S TYPE	She is a rich art investor.
TIME AND PLACE	Late 1980s; London Art scene.
SITUATION	Biddy tells the audience of her surprise when people started to treat her differently.

Biddy: I didn't at first understand what was happening. For someone like me, who was used to being tolerated, it came as a surprise. You see, before, everything I said was passed over. Well, smiled at, but the conversation would continue elsewhere. I was like the final touches of a well-decorated house. It gives pleasure, but you don't notice it. The sound of my voice was what mattered, it made people feel secure: England still had women who went to good schools and looked after large homes in the country, horses, dogs, children, that sort of thing, that was my voice. Tony – that's my first husband – said he found my conversation comforting background noise when he read the papers. But then, silences began to greet everything I said. Heavy silences. I thought there was something wrong.

Then I noticed they were waiting for more words, and these words had suddenly taken on a tremendous importance. But I was still saying the same things. You know, about shopping at Harrods and trains being slow, and good avocados being hard to come by, and cleaning ladies even harder. And then, I understood. You see, I had become tremendously rich. Not myself, but my husband, my second husband. And when you're that rich, nothing you do is trivial. If I took an hour telling a group of people how I had looked for and not found a good pair of gardening gloves, if I went into every detail of the weeks I had spent on this search, the phone bills I had run up, the catalogues I had returned, they were absolutely rivetted. Rivetted. Because it seemed everything I did, now that I was tremendously rich because of my second husband, mattered. Mattered tremendously. I hadn't expected this, because you see, my husband is foreign, Greek actually, and I found that not – well, not quite properly English, you know, to be married to a Greek – after all, Biddy *Andreas*? I could imagine my headmistress – we had a Greek girl at Benenden, we all turned down invitations to her island – and Yoyo – that's my husband, George, Yorgos, actually – he didn't even go to school here – but he was so rich and I became used to it – him, and me: being important.

NOTES FOR THIS SPEECH:

'Harrods': expensive London store.

'Benenden': expensive girls' school.

Your confidence grows as you tell of your journey from being insignificant to being important, and we should see this change in you: **See Note 4.**

You are talking to the audience: **See Note 6.**

33

KING HEDLEY II

August Wilson

FIRST PERFORMANCES	Pittsburgh 1999; New York 2001; London 2002
AWARDS	Nominated for the *Tony Award for Best Play*.
	Viola Davis **won** the *Tony Award for Best Featured Actress in a Play* **and** the *Drama Desk Award for Outstanding Featured Actress in a Play*.
CHARACTER	Tonya
PLAYED BY	Ella Joyce; Viola Davis [US]; Rakie Ayola [UK]
CHARACTER'S AGE	35
CHARACTER'S TYPE	King's wife.
TIME AND PLACE	1985; Pittsburgh, backyards of houses in the Hill District.
SITUATION	King's wife Tonya finds she is pregnant, but is determined not to have another child after having had Natasha when she was young.

Tonya: Why? Look at Natasha. I couldn't give her what she needed. Why I wanna go back and do it again? I ain't got nothing else to give. I can't give myself. How I'm gonna give her? I don't understand what to do . . . how to be a mother. You either love too much or don't love enough. Don't seem like there's no middle ground. I look up, she ten years old and I'm still trying to figure out life. Figure out what happened. Next thing I know she grown. Talking about she a woman. Just 'cause you can lay down and open your legs to a man don't make you a woman. I tried to tell her that. She's a baby! She don't know nothing about life. What she know? Who taught her? I'm trying to figure it out myself. Time I catch up it's moved on to something else. I got to watch her being thrown down a hole it's gonna take her a lifetime to crawl out and I can't do nothing to help her. I got to stand by and watch her. Why I wanna go back through all that?

I don't want to have a baby that younger than my grandchild. Who turned the world around like that? What sense that make? I'm thirty-five years old. Don't seem like there's nothing left. I'm through with babies. I ain't raising no more. Ain't raising no grandkids. I'm looking out for Tonya. I ain't raising no kid to have somebody shoot him. To have his friends shoot him. To have the police shoot him. Why I want to bring another life into this world that don't respect life? I don't want to raise no more babies when you got to fight to keep them alive. You take Little Buddy Will's mother up on Bryn Mawr Road. What she got? A heartache that don't never go away. She up there now sitting down in her living room. She got to sit down 'cause she can't stand up. She sitting down trying to figure it out. Trying to figure out what happened. One minute her house is full of life. The next minute it's full of death. She was waiting for him to come home and they bring her a corpse. Say, 'Come down and make the identification. Is this your son?' Got a tag on his toe say 'John Doe.' They got to put a number on it. John Doe number four. She got the dinner on the table. Say, 'Junior like fried chicken.' She got some of that. Say, 'Junior like string beans.' She got some of that. She don't know Junior ain't eating no more. He got a pile of clothes she washing up. She don't know Junior don't need no more clothes. She look in the closet. Junior ain't got no suit. She got to go buy him a suit. He can't try it on. She got to guess the size. Somebody come up and tell her, 'Miss So-and-So, your boy got shot.' She know before they say it. Her knees start to get weak. She shaking her head. She don't want to hear it. Somebody call the police. They come and pick him up off the sidewalk. Dead nigger on Bryn Mawr Road. They got to quit playing cards and come and pick him up. They used to take pictures. They don't even take pictures no more. They pull him out of the freezer and she look at him. She don't want to look. They make her look. What to do now? The only thing to do is call the undertaker. The line is busy. She got to call back five times. The undertaker got so much business he don't know what to do. He losing sleep. He got to hire two more helpers to go with the two he already got. He don't even look at the bodies no more. He couldn't tell you what they look like. He only remember the problems he have with them. This one so big and fat if he fall off the table it take six men to pick him up. That one ain't got no cheek. That one eyes won't stay closed. The other one been dead so long he got maggots coming out his nose.

The family can't pay for that one. The coroner wants to see the other one again. That one's mother won't go home. The other one . . . *[She stops to catch her breath.]* I ain't going through that. I ain't having this baby . . . and I ain't got to explain it to nobody.

NOTES FOR THIS SPEECH:

If it is too long for you, you could drop the first paragraph, or trim it to suit you: **See Note 2.**

The N word is unacceptable in some circumstances, so feel free to change it: **See Note 3.**

The varieties need to be as big as possible: **See Note 4.**

An Afro-American accent is needed to match the lines; it is not important that your skin colour does: **See Note 7.**

34

THE PAVILION

Craig Wright

FIRST PERFORMANCES	Pittsburgh 2000; New York 2005
AWARDS	Nominated for the *Drama Desk Award for Outstanding Play*.
CHARACTER	Kari
PLAYED BY	Kathryn Petersen; Jennifer Mudge
CHARACTER'S AGE	37
CHARACTER'S TYPE	She is the high school sweetheart, twenty years on.
TIME AND PLACE	The present; outside The Pavilion, an old dance hall in the fictional town of Pine City, Minnesota.
SITUATION	Kathryn is talking to her old boyfriend Peter, now a psychologist re-visiting his home town. Her husband Hans is a golf professional at the local club.

Kari: This morning, Hans was *inside* me, right?

Peter: Are you sure you –

Kari: – just listen, he was inside my *body*. If there's anybody else on earth I can tell this to, it's you. I get one life, right, and one body, and this morning Hans was inside it. And we were all finished, but he was still on top of me and I could tell he was thinking about something. So I said, like a dope, 'What are you thinking about?' And he said, 'A really difficult hole.' And it wasn't even a joke. That's what I live with. Me and that, alone every night in a split-level pro shop with beds for the human beings to rest on in between rounds! On a good day, it's bearable. On a bad day, you don't know. He's *so* mad, Peter. In his mind, he rescued me from the jaws of ill repute, right, because you'd dumped me and I'd had an abortion and 'oh God,' right, and he brought me out to be the Baroness Von Nine Iron of the most beautiful executive golf course in Becker County! And he *did* rescue me, kind of, see, that's the real problem, he did! And he was really sweet about it too, I mean, I can see his point, because I had been really lonely ever since you broke up with me, and Hans was so chivalrous about it, he took me out around town like it was all perfectly normal even though everybody always looked at us funny. One time he took me to The Voyager and he announced to the whole bar that we were getting married and he bought everyone a round of drinks. And Arne Neubeck was really drunk, like he always is, and he came over and said to Hans, 'You just made the biggest . . . fucking . . . mistake of your life.' And Hans punched him so fast and so hard, he knocked the wind out of that entire room and I got a dozen roses the next day from Arne with an apology. So Hans was really sweet, and he rescued me, and all he ever wanted from me in return, the way he sees it, all he ever wanted from me was a 'motherfucking baby' . . . and I wouldn't give him one, and *I won't give him one*, and his parents are all pissed off at me about it, but he's too nice to leave me and I can't change, it's just . . . *bad!* It's such an *awful, bad, home.*

NOTES FOR THIS SPEECH:

Peter has one embarrassed interruption: **See Note 1.**

Change the strong words if this is better for you: **See Note 3.**

Make sure you find all the varieties in the speech, so that it does not come over on one note. Make sure the end is really different to the beginning: **See Note 4.**

Find the happiness in the early memories (be pleased that you got those roses), so that the awfulness of the present state of the marriage can be experienced in all its horror: **See Note 5.**

40s

35

THE PLAY ABOUT THE BABY

Edward Albee

FIRST PERFORMANCES	London 1998; New York 2001
AWARDS	Marian Seldes nominated for the *Drama Desk Award for Outstanding Actress in a Play*.
CHARACTER	Woman
PLAYED BY	Frances de la Tour [UK]; Marian Seldes [US]
CHARACTER'S AGE	middle-aged
CHARACTER'S TYPE	She is an older woman.
TIME AND PLACE	Anytime; anywhere.
SITUATION	Three ages of women discuss women's themes, and interact together.

Woman: *[Looks at the audience.]* Well. I . . . uh . . . well, I suppose you'd like to know who I am, or why I'm here. *[Some uncertainty.]* Well, I'm with *him*; *[Gestures off left.]* that's why I'm here; I'm with him. The man; not the boy. The man indicated me as he exited, said 'Woman' and exited. Remember? That's why I'm here – to be with him. To help . . . *him*; to . . . assist *him. [Hand up, palm out, to abort protest.]* I'm not an actress; I want you to know that right off, though why you'd think I *was*, I mean automatically think I *was*, I don't know, though I *am* a trifle . . . theatrical, I suppose, and no apologies *there*. I *was* Prince Charming in our all-girl school production of *Snow White*, and while the bug may have bitten, it never took, *[Chuckles.]* Nor – and forgive the seeming discontinuity here – nor am I from the press. That's the first thing I want you to know – well, the second, actually, the first being . . . having been . . . . *[Trails off; starts again.]* Oh, I am a very good cook, among other things. I became that to please my husband, my *then* husband, who was in the habit of eating out, by which he meant . . . alone . . . without *me*. It occurred to *me* that if I . . . well, it was no good: Alone, to him, meant *specifically* not with *me*, though with others, with lots of others. And the great feasts I'd prepare . . . would be for *me*. Alone. I became quite heavy, which I no longer am, and unmarried, which I am to this day. I trust he is still eating alone . . . all by himself . . . facing a wall. *[Pause.]* No matter. Really: From the very first week, come dinnertime, he would put the paper under his arm, say 'Bye, bye,' or whatever, and . . . no matter. I *have* had journalistic dreams, though I am not a journalist – dreams of *being* a journalist, that is, and quite awake; not asleep. I went so far one time as to take a course; and my assignment was to interview a *writer*, to try to comprehend the 'creative mind' as they call it. *[Firm gesture.]* Don't try! Don't even give it a thought! There seems to be some sort of cabal going on on the part of these so-called creative people to keep the process a secret – a deep dark secret – from the rest of the world. What's the matter with these people? Do they think we're trying to steal their tricks? . . . would even *want* to!? And all I wanted to do was . . . under*stand*! And, let me tell you!, getting through to them – the creative types? – isn't easy. I mean even getting *at* them. I wrote politely to seven or eight of them, two poets, one biographer, a couple of short story writers, one female creator of 'theatre pieces,' etcetera, and not one of them answered. Silence; too busy 'creating,' I guess. *[On a roll now.]* I remember finally I bribed someone into giving me this one guy's agent's name – this novelist? – and persuaded the agent to call him and see if *I* could *call* him?, and maybe *talk* to him?, and finding out I could *do* that – with no guarantees, naturally – and calling, and hitting the brick wall of the novelist's male secretary. I don't *mean* anything by that, of course. *[Heavy wink.]* In any event, hitting *that* brick wall, having to repeat everything I'd said to the agent, and being told by the M.S. – the male secretary *[Heavy wink.]* – they'd get back to me, and waiting until finally they *did* – I mean, *really*, who did they think they were . . . *both* of them!? Finally, the M.S. *did* call me – I was in the touchy stages of a soufflée, naturally – telling me that *he* was there . . . *[Does fingers as quotes.]* 'Himself' that is: the famous novelist . . . and he *was* going to talk to me – 'himself' was – and I held the receiver to my ear, expecting what? – something other than a voice? I don't know – a choir of some sort? I held, and then his voice came . . . 'Here I am,' it said – *he* said – 'Here I am.' Odd, no? And the voice wasn't friendly, or unfriendly, gruffer than I'd thought it would be, perhaps, just . . . noncommittal. 'Here I am; I'm here.' I almost hung up, but I didn't. I mean, I'd gotten this close, and if I hung up who *knows* when I'd get another . . . *you* know. 'I'm here,' he said. And I rushed through what I wanted. 'I'm studying the creative process, and I want to do it with *you*, through *you* – watching *you*, understanding *you*.' 'You want to watch me while I *write*?!' he said, sort of incredulous, and I could sense the phone being passed back to the M.S., or just hung up, or tossed over his shoulder, or whatever. 'No! Wait!' I yelled. Silence. 'I'm waiting,' he finally said, no emotion at all. And I tried to explain what I really wanted.

NOTES FOR THIS SPEECH:

Although you are noted as 'middle-aged', Frances de la Tour was over 50 when she originated the role, and Marian Seldes was over 70 when she won her awards for the part.

If you need to do a shorter version, you could start half-way through with 'I have had journalistic dreams': **See Note 2.**

Find all the varieties you can, and end up in a different place to where you started: **See Note 4.**

You are talking to the audience: **See Note 6.**

36

DEATH AND THE MAIDEN

Ariel Dorfman

FIRST PERFORMANCES	London 1991; New York 1992
AWARDS	Won the *Laurence Olivier Award for Best New Play*.
	Juliet Stevenson **won** the *Laurence Olivier Award for Actress of the Year*.
	Glenn Close **won** the *Tony Award for Best Actress in a Play*; nominated for the *Drama Desk Award for Outstanding Actress in a Play*.
CHARACTER	Paulina
PLAYED BY	Juliet Stevenson [UK]; Glenn Close [US]
CHARACTER'S AGE	around 40
CHARACTER'S TYPE	She is a former revolutionary for democracy, raped and tortured for protecting the identity of her husband, now trying to cope with the results of that trauma.
TIME AND PLACE	Now; in a country that has just emerged from totalitarian dictatorship. The home of a former torture victim and her husband.
SITUATION	Thinking she has recognised the voice of a former torturer from 15 years before, Paulina has tied up a visitor to their house. She is arguing with her husband Gerardo about what to do with the hostage.

Paulina: When I heard his voice last night, the first thought that rushed through my head, what I've been thinking all these years, when you would catch me with a look that you said was – abstract, fleeting, right? – you know what I was thinking of? Doing to them, systematically, minute by minute, instrument by instrument, what they did to me. Specifically to him, to the doctor . . . Because the others were so vulgar, so – but he would play Schubert, he would talk about science, he even quoted Nietzche to me once.

Gerado: Nietzche.

Paulina: I was horrified at myself. That I should have such hatred in me, that I should want to do something like that to a defenceless human being, no matter how vile – but it was the only way to fall asleep at night, the only way of going out with you to cocktail parties in spite of the fact that I couldn't help asking myself if one of those present wasn't – perhaps not the exact same man, but one of those present might be . . . and so as not to go completely off my rocker and be able to deliver that Tavelli smile you say I'm going to have to continue to deliver – well, I would imagine pushing their head into a bucket of slime, or electricity, or when we would be making love and I could feel the possibility of an orgasm building, the very idea of currents going through my body would remind me and then – and then I had to simulate it, simulate it so you wouldn't know what I was thinking, so you wouldn't feel that it was your failure – oh Gerardo.

Gerado: Oh, my love, my love.

Paulina: So when I heard his voice, I thought the – only thing I want is to have him raped, have someone fuck him, so that he should know just once what it is to . . . And as I can't – I thought that it was a sentence that you would have to carry out.

Gerado: Don't go on, Paulina.

Paulina: But then I told myself it could be difficult, after all you do need to have a certain degree of enthusiasm to –

Gerado: Stop, Paulina

Paulina: So I asked myself if we could use a broom handle. Yes, Gerardo, you know, a broom. But I began to realise that wasn't what I really wanted. And you know what conclusion I came to, the only thing I really want?

[Brief pause.] I want him to confess. I want him to sit in front of that cassette-recorder and tell me what he did – not just to me, everything, to everybody – and then have him write it out in his own handwriting and sign it and I would keep a copy forever – with all the information, the names and data, all the details. That's what I want.

'Nietz[s]che': German philosopher, whose work was admired by Wagner and later by the Nazis; (usually pronounced 'Neechay');

'Tavelli': popular café in Santiago, Chile.

Paulina is 'around 40', and Juliet Stephenson was in her mid-30s when doing the role; Glenn Close was in her mid-40s.

You will need to act the other person's speeches: **See Note 1.**

You may want to soften the language a little: **See Note 3.**

The speech builds to a definite thought: **See Note 4.**

This piece does not need a specific accent, although using a slight one might be nice: **See Note 7.**

37

BETTY'S SUMMER VACATION

Christopher Durang

FIRST PERFORMANCES	New York 1999
AWARDS	Nominated for the *Drama Desk Award for Outstanding Play*.
	Kristine Neilson nominated for the *Drama Desk Award for Outstanding Featured Actress in a Play*.
CHARACTER	Mrs Siezmagraff
PLAYED BY	Kristine Neilson
CHARACTER'S AGE	mid-40s
CHARACTER'S TYPE	She is a lively vibrant woman, oblivious to anyone else's discomfort. She is also an emotionally anarchic landlady.
TIME AND PLACE	Now; nice seaside community – not a trendy chic location.
SITUATION	Betty is away on vacation with her friend Trudy, where life is like a series of lurid tabloid-style events. Trudy is put on 'trial' for the murder of a Mr Vanislaw, who she claims raped her. Her mother defends her, playing all the parts in the 'court'.

Mrs. Siezmagraff: *[Now as defense attorney.]* Mrs. Siezmagraff, did you know that your husband, Trudy's father, raped her repeatedly in her childhood? *[As herself; angry; her eyes flash.]* Did she tell you that? She's a liar!

I have to tell the truth, Trudy. *[As attorney.]* Mrs. Siezmagraff, is it not true that Trudy told you what was happening, and you refused to believe her? *[As herself.]*

She never told me. She never told me anything. I was a perfect mother. I don't know why she's telling these lies about me! *[As attorney.]* I call to the stand, Mrs. McGillicutty, your Irish housekeeper. *[As herself, baffled.]* I never had a housekeeper. I don't know who you're talking about. *[As attorney.]* Mrs. McGillicutty, you were in the employ of Mrs. Siezmagraff over there, were you not? *[Now she's the Irish maid, speaking with a very pronounced Irish accent.]* Oh, b'gosh and b'garin, yes, I worked for Mrs. Siezmagraff for many years. *[As herself.]* That's a lie! She's a liar! *[As attorney.]* Be quiet! Mrs. McGillicutty, can you prove to us that you worked for Mrs. Siezmagraff? *[As Irish maid.]* Oh yes, m'lord. Here are my pay stubs for my work for five years. *[As herself.]* Those are forgeries! I've never seen this woman before in my life! *[As Irish maid.]* B'gosh and b'garin, Mrs. Siezmagraff, don't you recognize me? I'm Kathleen. I come all the way from Killarney to be with your family and mind your little daughter, Trudy. *[As herself, getting hysterical.]* I've never seen you. You're a liar! Listen to her accent. She's not really Irish. *[As Irish maid; offended.]* I am Irish. And I worked for you for five years. Trudy remembers me, don't you, Trudy?

Trudy: Yeah . . . I remember you.

Mrs. Siezmagraff: *[As herself.]* Trudy, you're lying! *[As attorney.]* Don't be afraid of your mother, Trudy. Just tell the court the truth. *[As Irish maid.]* Oh, Trudy. Remember you and I spent many a happy hour. I would read you stories about the leprechauns and the funny mischief they would do. You remember, don't you, Trudy?

Trudy: Yes, Mrs McGillicutty.

Mrs. Siezmagraff: *[As attorney.]* Mrs. McGillicutty. Did you ever see Trudy's father molest her? *[As Irish maid.]* Yes, I did. *[As herself.]* She's lying! *[As attorney.]* And do you have any firsthand knowledge that Trudy's mother knew her husband was molesting Trudy? *[As Irish maid.]* Yes, I do. *[As herself, vicious and seething.]* That's not true! She's lying! *[As attorney.]* Mrs. McGillicutty, what is the knowledge you have? *[As Irish maid.]* On April 4th, 1978, Mrs. Siezmagraff said to me, 'I know my husband is raping my daughter, but I don't want to say anything to him, because I'm afraid he'd leave me.' *[As herself.]* You Irish pig! You liar! *[As Irish maid.]* And when she said that, I happened to be speaking into a tape recorder, making a transcription of my special Irish stew recipe, and so I have a recording of her admission on tape. So don't you be calling me a liar, Mrs. Siezmagraff. I'll take you to court and sue you for slander. *[MRS. SIEZMAGRAFF, caught by the Irish maid's evidence, now has full-fledged hysterics, and rushes center stage. As herself;*

hysterics.] It's true! It's true! I knew what was going on. And I didn't stop it. I was afraid I'd lose him. It's my fault Trudy was molested over and over and over, and no wonder she attacked Mr. Vanislaw. And I could've stopped Mr. Vanislaw's raping her, but I was drunk! I had had seven margaritas and I passed out. *[Weeps.]* I'm sorry, Trudy, I'm sorry – I ruined your life.

Trudy: Momma, momma!

Mrs. Siezmagraff: Don't convict my daughter! It's my fault. I didn't protect her. It's my fault. CONVICT ME, CONVICT ME! *[Collapses to the ground, weeps.]*

NOTES FOR THIS SPEECH:

This gives you a wonderful opportunity of playing three very different roles in the same speech.

It will be easy for you to cut or act Trudy's lines: **See Note 1.**

If it is too long for you, you could end it at an earlier point: **See Note 2.**

The different accents can either be very good, or not good at all; whatever is best for your situation: **See Note 7.**

38

PARK YOUR CAR IN THE HARVARD YARD

Israel Horovitz

FIRST PERFORMANCES	Los Angeles 1980; New York 1984
AWARDS	Judith Ivey nominated for the *Tony Award for Best Actress in a Play*.
CHARACTER	Kathleen
PLAYED BY	Barbara Babcock; Judith Ivey
CHARACTER'S AGE	around 40
CHARACTER'S TYPE	She is a quiet, mousy, strong-backed woman from Massachusetts, with a Boston accent.
TIME AND PLACE	Now; the Gloucester, Massachusetts home of an old teacher.
SITUATION	The meanest, hardest teacher has hired a house-keeper to look after him in his old age, and chosen a student he had flunked years earlier. She has gradually become fond of the old tyrant.

Kathleen: I had some really great news from Mrs. Dallin down at the High School. They're naming a prize for you. It's official: The Jacob Brackish Prize for Outstanding Scholarship in English Literature and Music Appreciation. Mrs. Dallin is workin' out the final details with Mick Verga, who's president of The Gloucester National Bank, now. Do ya' ba-leeeve that? If the graduate goes ta' Ha'vid, he or, she gets double. Great news, huh? *[She sings Paul Simon's song* 'Something So Right', *softly. BRACKISH is unresponsive. Her smile fades.]* They've all be'n callin', from ten towns around. You'd think it was the Pope himself that was sick, honest ta' God! Some of them wanted ta' run right over here now and give ya' their get-well-quick wishes in person, but, I told 'em all ta' wait till you're feelin' a bit less punk . . . *[Pause.]* Maybe I better call Dr. Chandler, huh? I won't let 'em take you to any hospital. I'll keep my promise on that, but, maybe he better come over and just have a look, huh? *[She stands and starts to the telephone. The rattle of Death rattles. BRACKISH dies. KATHLEEN turns around, in a sudden, looks across to him.]*

You say som'pin? *[She goes to BRACKISH; stares a while before realizing that he is dead. She 'crosses' herself.]* Oh God. Oh, God. Oh, God. Oh, God . . . *[KATHLEEN removes his glasses, 'closes his eyes.' She talks to BRACKISH as if to comfort him.]* You remember Snoddy Timmons from my year? He called, they all called: August Amoré, Franny and Evvie Farina, Harry and Margaret Budd, John Sharp, the Shimmas . . . God! Everybody! You're really respected around these parts, Jacob. You can't imagine. *[She sits holding his hand, watching him, waiting. They are both at peace. She smiles at BRACKISH. She holds his hand. She looks at him admiringly. She removes her locket.]* This was Mama's locket. My baby-picture's in one side. Mama, herself, is in the other . . . from when she was, ya' know, young. I was thinkin' you might want it. I've got other stuff of her's ta' keep for myself . . . *[Presses locket into his hand.]* Thanks, Mr. Brackish . . . Jacob. I'll always be grateful. *[KATHLEEN stands, listens to the music, just one brief moment; she speaks, softly, to a world.]* Pachelbel . . . 'Canon in D. Major' . . . 18th Century . . . Baroque . . . Beautiful. *[She walks to the telephone, dials the police station.]* Hullo . . . I wanna' report a death.

NOTES FOR THIS SPEECH:

'Ha'vid': Harvard University

The more friendly you are with him, the greater the surprise will be for us when he dies (and you must make this clear for the audience) It should also be a surprise that you have such a detailed knowledge of music: **See Note 5.**

You will need a New England accent for this: **See Note 7.**

Place the old man in a chair downstage of you, and the telephone even further downstage: **See Note 8.**

39

STRING OF PEARLS

Michele Lowe

FIRST PERFORMANCES	Pittsburgh 2003; New York 2004
AWARDS	Mary Testa nominated for the *Drama Desk Award for Outstanding Featured Actress in a Play.*
CHARACTER	Cindy
PLAYED BY	Sheila McKenna; Mary Testa
CHARACTER'S AGE	45
CHARACTER'S TYPE	She is a large overweight grave digger, and a lesbian.
TIME AND PLACE	Now; a graveyard, then a bar.
SITUATION	She tells the story of how her loneliness ended.

Lights up on CINDY. There is a large pile of dirt next to her. She holds a cellular phone.

Cindy: *[Into the phone.]* No, Mr. Krause, the daughter still hasn't arrived, we've been waiting over an hour. Yes, sir, I will, but there's a swan out here about half a row down. It's doing this thing where it comes toward me baring its teeth and then turns around. It's gone back and forth about ten times. What should I do, it keeps getting closer? Yes, sir. Thank you, sir. *[She hangs up.]* I fill in the grave and say a quick prayer. There is no one left to bury today and I have already raked the gravel paths. I had looked forward to having lunch with Mrs. Willow, my third-grade teacher who died last year – aisle 258, section 96, plot 7 – but it begins to rain so I take the rest of the day off. I dare myself to go to Wendy's. I gaze at the tables of five and six laughing women having lunch with their friends from work.

Every night I go to the bookstore and stare at women in the aisles. They turn and flee. I sit in the chairs for browsers and stay until closing. I read the books people have left behind. In the last week, I have read *How to Make Your Own Cannon*, a *Field Guide to Mushrooms*, *Attila King of the Huns* and *The Life and Lyrics of Sir Edward Dyer*.

I have a card printed with my name and phone number and have dropped it into every Dostoevsky and Faulkner on the shelves. I've left fliers with my name on it in the bathroom at Starbucks. But nobody calls. Not a single person. I am looking for a woman, but no one is looking for me.

I go to O'Donaghue's for a nightcap. Jerry gives me a beer and then I see her down at the end of the bar. What creature sits before me? What soul from heaven has found me on earth? I cannot take my eyes off this woman.

[They look at each other. The next night:]

Oh my God, she's getting off her stool. Oh my God, she's coming over. She's going to –

Beth: Hello.

Cindy: Her elbow grazes my right pinkie. Every pore in my body explodes.

Beth: She has nice lips and smells like chocolate.

Cindy: She tells me her name is Beth. She's fifteen years older than me, maybe twenty. Maybe twenty-five. Oh fuck it, she's ancient, but I don't care.

NOTES FOR THIS SPEECH:

The speeches by Beth are easy to cover, and you can indicate or speak 'the next night': See Note 1.

Feel free to change the words to suit your purposes: See Note 3.

We should think Mrs. Willow was a contemporary friend until 'who died last year': See Note 5.

It would be fine to use a real cell phone: See Note 9.

40

RECKLESS

Craig Lucas

FIRST PERFORMANCES	New York 1988, 2004
AWARDS	Nominated for the *Drama Desk Award for Outstanding New Play*.
	Robin Bartlett nominated for the *Drama Desk Award for Outstanding Actress in a Play*.
	Mary-Louise Parker nominated for the *Tony Award for Best Actress in a Play*.
CHARACTER	Rachel
PLAYED BY	Robin Bartlett, Mary-Louise Parker
CHARACTER'S AGE	40s
CHARACTER'S TYPE	She is a perpetually perky American housewife.
TIME AND PLACE	Today, Christmas; the pay phone at a gas station in the suburbs.
SITUATION	Rachel is at a pay phone in her robe and slippers, having fled her home and her husband Tom. There is snow on the ground.

Rachel: Jeanette? Rachel. Merry Christmas. . . . No, everything's great, but listen, would you and Freddie mind taking a little spin down here to the Arco station at Route 3 and Carl Bluestein Boulevard? No, no, nothing like that, I just came outside. . . . Oh, isn't it? It's beautiful, uh-huh, listen, Jeanette, Tom took a . . . Tom. . . . It's so ridiculous. He took a contract out on my life. . . . A contract? . . . Uh-huh. Right. And, I mean, the man broke in downstairs so I thought I'd better go out of the house, so I climbed out over the garage and I was afraid to ring your bell, because you have all those pretty lights and I was afraid he might be following my tracks in the snow – *[LLOYD approaches in the darkness.]* – and so I thought maybe you'd just zip down here and we'd all have some eggnog or something, what do you say? . . . Jeane –? No. . . . No, I know, I am, I'm a kidder. . . . But – Merry Christmas to you too, Jeanette, please don't . . . *[JEANETTE has hung up. RACHEL turns: sees LLOYD, screams.]*

AAAAAAGH! NO, MY GOD! PLEASE!

Lloyd: Hey. Hey.

Rachel: Oh, I'm sorry. Did you want to use the phone? Please, go right ahead.

Lloyd: I'm just trying to find a gas station.

Rachel: This is a gas station, right here, you found one. For *gas!* Oh, not on Christmas Eve, maybe up on the turnpike . . . Merry Christmas.

NOTES FOR THIS SPEECH:

You can act the other speeches easily: **See Note 1.**

Make sure you surprise the audience with the news of a contract on you; you will also get a good contrast if you are worried about where Lloyd might find gas, but happily wish him Merry Christmas: **See Note 5.**

Since you will be playing the telephone call out front, make sure Lloyd approaches you from alongside, so we all see your reaction to him: **See Note 8.**

You could just put a robe over your clothes, to get the effect: **See Note 9.**

1

IRON

Rona Munro

FIRST PERFORMANCES	Edinburgh 2002; London 2003; New York 2003
AWARDS	Sandy McDade **won** the *Evening Standard Theatre Award for Best Actress*.
CHARACTER	Fay
PLAYED BY	Sandy McDade [UK]; Lisa Emery [US]
CHARACTER'S AGE	45
CHARACTER'S TYPE	She is erratic and impetuous.
TIME AND PLACE	Now; Interview room, women's prison in the UK.
SITUATION	Fay is serving a life sentence for murdering her husband with a kitchen knife. Her daughter Josie, who was 11 at the time and who has not seen her mother for 15 years, decides one day to visit.

Fay: We had a row. I don't remember what about . . . but after we'd stopped he was fine and I was raging. We'd had a few but not that many, enough so I can never remember all of it.

I was just sitting, just sitting in my chair like a coal burning in the fire, so full of anger I couldn't move. I felt like I was scorching my own clothes but I never made a sound. He said 'Ach there's no talking to you . . .' So he didn't. He drank a beer. He watched a bit of television. He read the paper and laughed at the sports news . . .

I just sat.

Once he looked at me and sort of snorted through his nose in disgust. 'Aren't you going to bed?' he said.

I said nothing. I just sat. Burning.

He had another beer. He fell asleep and snored with the telly lighting up his face, mouth open.

I sat and looked at him.

I felt that no-one could ever waste so much love on anyone.

I felt so full of crying that I was just tight with tears, from my toes to my hair, stretched tight with crying that wouldn't come out, I sat there for hours and I remembered. And what I remembered, what I couldn't stop remembering, was a moment when we are arguing when my anger flashed over and started to burn me alive and that was the moment he laughed at me. He set me on fire and watched me burn and he laughed.

Then the strangest thing happened. I felt my lips pull back from my teeth in a snarl like a dog's. I tried to close my mouth but my lips kept twitching and tugging away from my teeth. I bared my teeth like a wolf. Like a demon. My eyes felt like they were popping out.

I felt there was a devil in me.

I felt I was the devil.

I think I was the devil then, or his dog.

I had a kitchen knife in my hand. I don't remember picking it up but it was in my hand.

I stuck it in him.

The stupid fuck, thinking he could just do or say anything he wanted and then snore away as if what he made me feel had no consequences at all. The stupid fuck.

You'd think he would've woken up more. Maybe we'd had more than I knew.

For two seconds I was glad when I saw him bleed. Then I just wished that none of it had ever happened at all.

I miss him so much. I miss him so much. I wish I'd never met him to hurt him so. You should remember your Dad. He loved you.

You should remember your Dad and go away from here and never come back.

Go away! *[She starts shoving JOSIE, hitting her.]* Go away Josie! Leave me alone!

NOTES FOR THIS SPEECH:

Feel free to change the strong language to suit your needs: **See Note 3.**

Acting out the murder will give you a lot of varieties. There is a huge build-up from starting sitting next to your husband, to sticking the knife in him: **See Note 4.**

The Scottish accent works well for this piece, but if you need to change accents, then change the Scottish 'Ach' to 'Oh': **See Note 7.**

Your daughter can be downstage one side of you, and your husband the other side: **See Note 8.**

42

VIRGINIA

Edna O'Brien

FIRST PERFORMANCES	Stratford, Ontario 1980; London 1981; New York 1985
AWARDS	Maggie Smith nominated for the *Laurence Olivier Award for Best Actress of the Year in a New Play*.
CHARACTER	Virginia
PLAYED BY	Maggie Smith [Canada and UK]; Kate Nelligan [US]
CHARACTER'S AGE	40s
TYPE	Virginia Woolf was a famous writer – fluent, iconoclastic, vulnerable, savage, high-minded, low-minded, and intermittently insane.
TIME AND PLACE	1920s; England – the life and writings of Virginia Woolf in an abstract setting.
SITUATION	Virginia is telling Man (all the men in her life) how it was when she was young.

Virginia: I dreamt that I leant over the edge of the boat and fell down, I went under the sea, I have been dead and yet am now alive again – it was awful, awful, and as before waking, the voices of the birds and the sound of wheels chime and chatter in a queer harmony, grow louder and louder and the sleeper feels himself drawing towards the shores of life, the sun growing hotter, cries sounding louder, something tremendous about to happen.

Man: Ginny – Virginia!

Virginia: Moments, moments of my being . . . in here, captive. I shall scrape the sea-bed clean. My father bent over his tomes . . . no light lover he, no superficial optimist, one of the giant breed, alone in the ice-bound seas.

My two bloods dashing together. My fath€
oarsman, coach of oarsmen. And my mother's o
His wife my mother. When she was presidin,
very stirring, the room full of people, her several chil€
high and plates and plates of innocent bread and but
Life and a little strip of time presented itself to her €
took a look at life, and she had a clear sense of it, som
private which she shared neither with her children nor .
always trying to get the better of it as it was of her and som€
she felt this thing called Life terrible, hostile and quick to poun
she said brandishing her sword 'Nonsense.'

Yes I wanted her to myself, one does. I wanted to be singled €
her my little stories about souls flying about looking for bodies. Sr
mother, his wife, not at all the same thing. It must be a strange th
and wife, all that copulation. Marriage and motherhood without aw€
is not enough. Rather crowded and rather anxious and very valiant €
enough. Her pride in him was like the pride of one in some lofty mou¡
visited only by the light of the stars, noble, yes, enthusiastic, yes, but hur¡
humble. My mother. One says it. One cannot not say it. A single phrase,
voice, or that beautiful figure so upright in the ground, in her long shabby
the head held high, so upright and so distinct and the eyes that looked str€
ahead, hurrying saying,

'Come along, quick, quick, don't keep Father waiting.'

Or sitting there writing a letter at the table, and the silver candlesticks
and the high carved chair and the three cornered brass inkpot and then not
there.

She was upstairs and my half-brother, George Duckworth took me into her
bedroom to kiss her goodbye and she said, 'Hold yourself straight my little goat.'
It was May the fifth, eighteen ninety five.

It was about six in the morning. I saw the doctor walk away, I saw the pigeons
floating, settling.

They wrapped towels around me and gave me brandy, I think the sun was
coming up. She had just died.

Death plays havoc.

NOTES

'tomes'
'parley
You d
Feel
Not¡
Giv
ab
N
N

ɔooks;

d': discussed.

not really hear the other speech: **See Note 1.**

ee to trim this story of your mother's death to suit your circumstances: **See** 2.

a different quality to how you talk about your father, to how you do the same ut your mother: **See Note 4.**

ke sure you place him so that we can see you with all your thought changes: **See**)te 8.

From VIRGINIA by Edna O'Brien, published by Hogarth Press. Reprinted by permission of The Random House Group Ltd.

43

A KIND OF ALASKA

Harold Pinter

FIRST PERFORMANCES	London 1982; New York 1984
AWARDS	Judi Dench **won** the *Evening Standard Theatre Award for Best Actress.*
CHARACTER	Deborah
PLAYED BY	Judi Dench [UK]; Dianne Wiest [US]
CHARACTER'S AGE	mid-40s
CHARACTER'S TYPE	She thinks she is a teenager, but she is in the body of a much older woman.
TIME AND PLACE	1980s; a long-stay hospital anywhere.
SITUATION	A middle-aged woman wakes up after 30 years passed in a coma induced by sleeping sickness. In her mind she is still 16. She is talking to Hornby her doctor, and her sister Pauline.

Deborah: Now what was I going to say? *[She begins to flick her cheek, as if brushing something from it.]*

Now what –? Oh dear, oh no. Oh dear. *[Pause.]*

Oh dear. *[The flicking of her cheek grows faster.]*

Yes, I think they're closing in. They're closing in. They're closing the walls in. Yes. *[She bows her head, flicking faster, her fingers now moving about over her face.]*

Oh . . . well . . . oooohhhhh . . . oh no . . . oh no . . . *[During the course of this speech her body becomes hunchbacked.]*

Let me out. Stop it. Let me out. Stop it. Stop it. Stop it. Shutting the walls on me. Shutting them down on me. So tight, so tight. Something panting, something panting. Can't see. Oh, the light is going. The light is going. They're shutting up shop. They're closing my face. Chains and padlocks. Bolting me up. Stinking.

The smell. Oh my goodness, oh dear, oh my goodness, oh dear, I'm so young. It's a vice. I'm in a vice. It's at the back of my neck. Ah. Eyes stuck. Only see the shadow of the tip of my nose. Shadow of the tip of my nose. Eyes stuck. *[She stops flicking abruptly, sits still. Her body straightens. She looks up. She looks at her fingers, examines them.]*

Nothing. *[Silence. She speaks calmly, is quite still.]*

Do you hear a drip? *[Pause.]*

I hear a drip. Someone's left the tap on. *[Pause.]*

I'll tell you what it is. It's a vast series of halls. With enormous interior windows masquerading as walls. The windows are mirrors, you see. And so glass reflects glass. For ever and ever. *[Pause.]*

You can't imagine how still it is. So silent I hear my eyes move. *[Silence.]*

I'm lying in bed. People bend over me, speak to me. I want to say hullo, to have a chat, to make some inquiries. But you can't do that if you're in a vast hall of glass with a tap dripping. *[Silence. She looks at PAULINE.]*

I must be quite old. I wonder what I look like. But it's of no consequence. I certainly have no intention of looking into a mirror. *[Pause.]*

No. *[She looks at HORNBY.]*

You say I have been asleep. You say I am now awake. You say I have not awoken from the dead. You say I was not dreaming then and am not dreaming now. You say I have always been alive and am alive now. You say I am a woman. *[She looks at PAULINE, then back at HORNBY.]*

She is a widow. She doesn't go to her ballet classes any more. Mummy and Daddy and Estelle are on a world cruise. They've stopped off in Bangkok. It'll be my birthday soon. I think I have the matter in proportion. *[Pause.]*

Thank you.

NOTES FOR THIS SPEECH:

This gives you the opportunity of playing both a young girl and a middle-aged woman; make the differences clear (especially in the last part, where your sister is either a young girl or middle-aged to you): **See Note 5.**

You can play this sitting on a chair; establish the other two so we can see you looking to one side and then the other: **See Note 8.**

44

WHEN SHE DANCED

Martin Sherman

FIRST PERFORMANCES	New York 1990; London 1991
AWARDS	Marcia Jean Kurtz nominated for the *Drama Desk Award for Outstanding Featured Actress in a Play*.
	Frances de la Tour **won** the *Laurence Olivier Award for Best Actress in a Supporting Role*.
CHARACTER	Miss Belzer
PLAYED BY	Marcia Jean Kurtz [US]; Frances de la Tour [UK]
CHARACTER'S AGE	early 40s
CHARACTER'S TYPE	She is plain and shy, employed as a Russian interpreter between the famous dancer Isadora Duncan and her Russian contacts.
TIME AND PLACE	1923; a house on the rue de la Pompe, Paris.
SITUATION	Miss Belzer is explaining why she stayed with the eccentric Isadora.

Miss Belzer: I saw her dance. I was very young, perhaps twenty. It was her first tour of Russia – in St. Petersburg. We had heard about this strange creature from America who danced barefoot on an empty platform, wearing only a tunic, and behaving – well, they said in very strange ways. The audience was there, I think, to laugh. When she first appeared they made noises – you know, hissing noises. She was standing. Simply standing. Standing still. The music was playing. It was – I think – Chopin. And then – very slowly – she began to move. But it was not the way anyone else moved on a stage. I do not know exactly *what* it was – I think perhaps she simply walked from one side of the stage to another – and then it was hard for me to see, because my eyes were burning – that is what happens when I cry – but I do not know why I was crying. I thought I saw children dancing, but there were no children. I thought I saw the face of my mother as she lay dying. I thought I remembered the rabbi's words. I thought I was kissing my child before they took him away from me. I thought I felt the lips, the lips of a man in a great white hat on the train to Kiev – and all she was doing on the stage was walking, just a few steps up, a few steps down, but this walk of hers, it was like a comet shooting through my body – and then, suddenly, she stopped – that was it – it was over – and the audience that had been making those noises, this hissing, were on their feet, cheering, but my eyes were still burning. And this is why I do not like to cry. And I never cry since that night – since eighteen years. No matter what has happened, I never cry. But sometimes when sleep does not come or when the dreams have frightened me – sometimes . . . then . . . I make myself think of Isadora – dancing!

NOTES FOR THIS SPEECH:

Make sure that your memories of your child, of your mother etc. have different emotions for you: See Note 4.

Find different ways of reacting to the memory of Isadora: See Note 5.

You are talking to the audience: See Note 6.

The way it is written suggests an accent. You can play this with any accent, foreign or not: See Note 7.

45

BROADWAY BOUND

Neil Simon

FIRST PERFORMANCES	New York 1986; London 1991
AWARDS	Nominated for the *Tony Award for Best Play*, and the *Drama Desk Award for Outstanding New Play*. Linda Lavin **won** the *Tony Award for Best Actress in a Play*, **and** the *Drama Desk Award for Outstanding Actress in a Play*.
CHARACTER	Kate
PLAYED BY	Linda Lavin [US]; Anna Massey [UK]
CHARACTER'S AGE	40s
CHARACTER'S TYPE	She is a middle-aged Jewish wife.
TIME AND PLACE	1950s; a family home in Brighton Beach, just outside New York City.
SITUATION	She has found out that her husband Jack has kept a friendship with the woman he had had an affair with, and for which she had previously forgiven him. This discovery breaks up their relationship.

Kate: What do *I* want to do? Is that how it works? You have an affair, and I get the choice of forgetting about it or living alone for the rest of my life? . . . It's so simple for you, isn't it? I am so angry. I am so hurt by your selfishness. You break what was good between us and leave me to pick up the pieces . . . and *still* you continue to lie to me.

Jack: I told you everything.

Kate: I knew about that woman a year ago. I got a phone call from a friend, I won't even tell you who . . . 'What's going on with you and Jack?' she asks me. 'Are you two still together? Who's this woman he's having lunch with every day?' she asks me . . . I said, 'Did you see them together?' . . . She said, 'No, but I heard' . . . I said 'Don't believe what you hear. Believe what you see!' and I hung up on her . . . Did I do good, Jack? Did I defend my husband like a good wife? . . . A year I lived with that, hoping to God it wasn't true and if it was, praying it would go away . . . And God was good to me. No more phone calls, no more stories about Jack and his lunch partner . . . No more wondering why you were coming home late from work even when it wasn't busy season . . . Until this morning. Guess who calls me? . . . Guess who Jack was having lunch with in the same restaurant twice last week? . . . Last year's lies don't hold up this year, Jack . . . This year you have to deal with it.

Jack: . . . It's true. I saw her last week. Twice in the same restaurant, once in another restaurant.

Kate: And where else, Jack? Do you always sit or do you lie down once in a while? *[Rising.]* Twice tonight I went to the phone to see if you were really working, but I was so afraid to hear that you left early, I couldn't dial the number . . . How is it possible I could hate you so much after loving you all my life?

NOTES FOR THIS SPEECH:

You can either ignore the other speeches, or incorporate them into your lines: **See Note 1.**

You build to the terrible climax of telling him you hate him: **See Note 4.**

Although in the original you are seated for a while, in your version you can move around whenever you want; and make sure he is downstage of you: **See Note 8.**

46

HOW I LEARNED TO DRIVE

Paula Vogel

FIRST PERFORMANCES	New York 1997; London 1998
AWARDS	Won *The Pulitzer Prize for Drama*, and the *Drama Desk Award for Outstanding New Play*.
CHARACTER	Aunt Mary
PLAYED BY	Johanna Day [US]; Jenny Galloway [UK]
CHARACTER'S AGE	40s
CHARACTER'S TYPE	She is a typical housewife.
TIME AND PLACE	Today; Maryland.
SITUATION	The wife of a paedophile shows her blindness as to what her husband Peck was really up to, as he slowly groomed his niece to be his next victim.

Aunt Mary: My husband was such a good man – is. Is such a good man. Every night, he does the dishes. The second he comes home, he's taking out the garbage, or doing yard work, lifting the heavy things I can't. Everyone in the neighborhood borrows Peck – it's true – women with husbands of their own, men who just don't have Peck's abilities – there's always a knock on our door for a jump start on cold mornings, when anyone needs a ride, or help shoveling the sidewalk – I look out, and there Peck is, without a coat, pitching in.

I know I'm lucky. The man works from dawn to dusk. And the overtime he does every year – my poor sister. She sits every Christmas when I come to dinner with a new stole, or diamonds, or with the tickets to Bermuda.

I know he has troubles. And we don't talk about them. I wonder, sometimes, what happened to him during the war. The men who fought World War II didn't have 'rap sessions' to talk about their feelings. Men in his generation were expected to be quiet about it and get on with their lives. And sometimes I can feel him just fighting the trouble – whatever has burrowed deeper than the scar tissue – and we don't talk about it. I know he's having a bad spell because he comes looking for me in the house, and just hangs around me until it passes. And I keep my banter light – I discuss a new recipe, or sales, or gossip – because I think domesticity can be a balm for men when they're lost. We sit in the house and listen to the peace of the clock ticking in his well-ordered living room, until it passes.

[Sharply.] I'm not a fool. I know what's going on. I wish you could feel how hard Peck fights against it – he's swimming against the tide, and what he needs is to see me on the shore, believing in him, knowing he won't go under, he won't give up –

And I want to say this about my niece. She's a sly one, that one is. She knows exactly what she's doing; she's twisted Peck around her little finger and thinks it's all a big secret. Yet another one who's borrowing my husband until it doesn't suit her anymore.

Well. I'm counting the days until she goes away to school. And she manipulates someone else. And then he'll come back again, and sit in the kitchen while I bake, or beside me on the sofa when I sew in the evenings. I'm a very patient woman. But I'd like my husband back.

I am counting the days.

NOTES FOR THIS SPEECH:

'rap sessions': sessions of talking with a psychiatrist

The darker the mood you are in when you want your husband back, the lighter the mood you can hit on when you are counting the days for him to return. Sudden changes work really well, between talking of your husband, and then of your niece: **See Note 5.**

You are talking to the audience: **See Note 6.**

47

NOT ABOUT NIGHTINGALES

Tennessee Williams

FIRST PERFORMANCES	London 1998; New York 1999
AWARDS	Nominated for the *Tony Award for Best Play*, and the *Drama Desk Award for Outstanding Play*. Corin Redgrave [Warden] nominated for the *Tony Award for Best Actor in a Play* and the *Drama Desk Award for Outstanding Actor in a Play*. Finbar Lynch [Jim] nominated for the *Tony Award for Best Actor in a Featured Role in a Play* and the *Drama Desk Award for Outstanding Actor in a Play*.
CHARACTER	Mrs Bristol
PLAYED BY	Sandra Searles Dickinson [UK and US]
CHARACTER'S AGE	late 40s
CHARACTER'S TYPE	She is a worn matron, dressed in black.
TIME AND PLACE	1938; the Warden's office in a prison.
SITUATION	The mother of Jack, an inmate, is asking Warden Whalen about her son, since she has been sent a letter telling her Jack has been certified insane. The play has waited 60 years before its first performance, and is based on a true incident, when protesting prisoners were locked in a boiler room, four of them broiled to death, and the others were badly affected.

Mrs. Bristol: Jack's last letter was strange. I – I have it with me. It's not at all like Jack. He wasn't transferred to any other prison, was he? Because he kept complaining all through his letter about how terribly hot it was in a place called Klondike. His penmanship has always been quite irregular but this was so bad I could scarcely read it at all – I thought possibly he wasn't well when he wrote it – feverish, you know – he's very subject to colds especially this time of year. I – I brought this wool comforter with me. For Jack. I know it's not easy, Mr. Whalen, to make exceptions in an institution like this. But in Jack's case where there are so many, *many* considerations – so much that I regret *myself* when I look back at things – Mistakes that I made –

Warden: Mistakes, yes, we all make mistakes.

Mrs. Bristol: Such *grave* mistakes, Mr. Whalen. Our household was not an altogether happy one, you see. Jack's father – well, he was a Methodist minister and his views naturally differed quite a bit from most young boys' –

Warden: A preacher's son?

Mrs. Bristol: Yes! But there was a disagreement among the congregation not long ago and my husband was forced to retire.

Warden: I see. I'm very busy, I – Have you found that card?

Jim: Not yet.

Mrs. Bristol: He was so – so uncompromising, even with poor Jack. So Jack left home. Of course it was against my wishes but – *[She opens her bag and produces sheaf of letters.]* Oh, those long marvelous letters that he wrote! If you would only read them you'd see for yourself what an exceptional boy Jack was. Port Said, Marseilles, Cairo, Shanghai, Bombay! 'Oh, mother, it's so big, so terribly, terribly big,' he kept on writing. As though he'd tried to squeeze it in his heart until the bigness of it made this heart crack open! Look! These envelopes! You see they're packed so full that he could hardly close them! Pictures of places, too! Elephants in India. They're used like packhorses, he said, for common labor. Little Chinese junkets have square sails. They scoot about like dragonflies on top of the water. The bay at Rangoon. Here's where the sun comes up like thunder, he wrote on the back of this one! Kipling, you know – I wrote him constantly – 'Jack, there's no advancement in it. A sailor's always a sailor. Get out of it, son. Get into the Civil Service!' He wrote me back – 'I kept the middle watch last night. You see more stars down here than in the northern water. The Southern Cross is right above me now, but won't be long – because our course is changing –' I stopped opposing then, I thought that anything he loved as much as that would surely keep him safe. And then he didn't write a while – until this came. I still can't understand it!

NOTES FOR THIS SPEECH:

'Where the sun comes up like thunder': quote from Rudyard Kipling's poem *Road to Mandalay*.

You can easily act out the speeches by the other characters, as long as we know it was your husband who was so uncompromising: **See Note 1.**

You can cut the middle speeches if the piece is too long for you: **See Note 2.**

Find the happiness in Jack's letters, to give good variations: **See Note 4.**

You could always use a real handbag and letters: **See Note 9.**

over 50s

48

THE TALE OF THE ALLERGIST'S WIFE

Charles Busch

FIRST PERFORMANCES	New York 2000
AWARDS	Nominated for the *Drama Desk Award for Outstanding New Play*, and the *Tony Award for Best Play*.
	Linda Lavin nominated for the *Drama Desk Award for Outstanding Actress in a Play*, and the *Tony Award for Best Actress in a Play*.
CHARACTER	Marjorie
PLAYED BY	Linda Lavin
CHARACTER'S AGE	50s
CHARACTER'S TYPE	She is the wife of a philanthropic allergist; an attractive stylish woman. She speaks in a somewhat studied manner.
TIME AND PLACE	Now; two-bedroom apartment on Manhattan's Upper West Side.
SITUATION	Marjorie is in the throes of an epic depression – not quiet, but a raging frustration. Her mother Frieda has come round to 'help', and has just told her that she is bored.

Marjorie: This is so simplistic and insulting. You don't know anything about me. We are strangers!

Frieda: Get off your duff, get dressed and do some volunteer work. Make yourself useful.

Marjorie: Volunteer work. I should do some volunteer work. I am the Queen of volunteer work, Mother. A Brigadier General in the army of volunteer workers. For God's sake. What do you think I've been doing for the past thirty years? Planned Parenthood, Dance Theatre of Harlem. I gave my life's blood to the Lenox Hill Hospital Thrift Shop. Every week, I was in that back room on my hands and knees unpacking every filthy box, sorting through garments stiff from sweat and urine. Every day I saw the other volunteers ransack the shop for any rag with a designer label. Then by chance, buried in a box of moldy paperbacks, I discover a first edition hardcover English translation of 'Siddartha' in mint condition, still with the original dust jacket, and personally inscribed by Hermann Hesse. I put it aside making it abundantly clear to everyone that I intended to buy it myself. 'To buy,' that is the operative phrase here. I come back the next day. 'Where's my book? Where is 'Siddartha'?' The manager, Libby Fleishman, says 'Oh, I'm so sorry. I forgot that you put that aside. I sold it to a dealer.' It was an act of deliberate cruelty. I went to the hospital board and exposed Libby's operation of selling directly to antique dealers and getting a personal cut. They demanded proof but none of the other volunteers would back me up. I was humiliated, disgraced and betrayed. So yes, Mother, I have done my share of volunteer work. I have chopped the vegetables, driven the meals on wheels, registered people for the vote, made puppets for the retarded, pushed the hospital cart, stuffed the mailing, licked the envelopes, worked the hotline, sewn the quilt, saved the whales, served everyone's needs but my own. Well, what about my needs, Mother? Who's gonna volunteer to save me?

NOTES FOR THIS SPEECH:

'allergist': physician specializing in the diagnosis and treatment of allergies;

'Sidd[h]artha': book by Herman Hesse about an Indian contemporary of the Buddha; it is the story of a man who spends his entire life in search of truth and self-understanding.

It will be easy for you to let us know what your mother says: See Note 1.

There is a long list of the various things you have done for charity, so don't hesitate to make it a big build: See Note 4.

49

PRIN

Andrew Davies

FIRST PERFORMANCES	London 1989; New York 1990
AWARDS	Sheila Hancock nominated for the *Laurence Olivier Award for Actress of the Year*.
CHARACTER	Prin
PLAYED BY	Sheila Hancock [UK]; Eileen Atkins [US]
CHARACTER'S AGE	over 50
CHARACTER'S TYPE	She is the Principal of a teachers' training college, egocentric and eccentric, her noble ideals doomed by her arrogant insensitivity.
TIME AND PLACE	England today; main lecture hall of the college.
SITUATION	She is talking to prospective students.

Prin: *[To the audience.]* It's very gratifying to see you here in such large numbers at our Open Day. We like to offer prospective students, and the parents of prospective students, the opportunity of seeing and experiencing what we are about here. I am the Principal of this college. That's Principal with an A L at the end, not an L E. I say this because when it is time for you to make your applications, the more illiterate amongst you will favour the latter spelling. Those applications will of course go straight into the waste-paper basket. However, they do unconsciously reveal a certain truth. I do embody a principle. That principle is the pursuit of excellence. It's quite unfamiliar to most of you of course. I fully realize that you're leading lives of quite mind-numbing mediocrity, using perhaps a tenth or a twentieth of the human potential you were born with. And you feel guilty about that, of course, and resentful that you're being reminded of it. It's in the interest of the system that you should feel like that, and stay in that benighted state. I am interested in transforming society. My graduates bloom like terrifying exotic flowers in classrooms all over the country, showing the children how to be extraordinary, as I have shown them to be extraordinary. The power for extraordinary change exists in every human being. Think what it could be like to allow yourselves to be wholly known. Well: I shan't take up any more of my valuable time. I have people to bully. I have plots to put down. Try to understand the essence of this place. It's not an ordinary place. And then, perhaps, I shall meet some of you next year as first-year students, when I shall take great pleasure in terrifying the wits out of you and changing your lives. Good-afternoon. *[She turns her back and walks upstage.]*

NOTES FOR THIS SPEECH:

'benighted': backward, unenlightened.

Avoid getting trapped into giving all the speech on one note: See Note 4.

Find a different tone for your last 'changing your lives': See Note 5.

You use the audience as if they were the students: See Note 6.

50

LAUGHING WILD

Christopher Durang

FIRST PERFORMANCES	New York 1987; London 1988
AWARDS	E. Katherine Kerr nominated for the *Drama Desk Award for Outstanding Actress in a Play*.
CHARACTER	Woman
PLAYED BY	E. Katherine Kerr [US]; Amanda Hillwood [UK]
CHARACTER'S AGE	over 50
CHARACTER'S TYPE	She is highly intelligent and sardonic; and has been institutionalized in the past.
TIME AND PLACE	Now; New York.
SITUATION	She is telling about her past skirmishes with American urban life, and mental breakdowns.

Woman: I wish I had been killed when I was a fetus. It wasn't legal then, and my mother didn't think of it, but I think she'd prefer I'd never been born. I know I'd prefer she'd never have been born, and that would have taken care of my not being born as well. Plus, I'm really sick of Mother Theresa, aren't you? I mean, what makes her such a saint? She's just like Sally Jessy Raphael, only different. Oh, God, I'm starting to ramble. But I can't help it. And what does the A.A. prayer say? God help me to accept the things I cannot change. I can't change my rambling. Plus I'm not an alcoholic anyway; I just went there because I didn't know what else to do with my life, and I thought if I told them all I was an alcoholic they'd accept me. But it didn't help. They say if you don't believe in God, you just have to believe in a Higher Power than yourself, but that didn't help me particularly. I mean, who? Phil Donahue? Mother Theresa? The god Dionysus?

And there was this woman at A.A. who came and said she had stopped drinking but her life hadn't been working out anyway, and how her parents were alcoholics too, and she seemed very intense and kind of crazy, and it was hard to look at her because she was missing a tooth right in front, it didn't make for an attractive package at all; and she talked about how the program had helped her realize she was powerless over alcohol, and this seemed to make her happy for some reason or other, although I think I'm powerless over lots of things and it doesn't make me happy; and then I shouted out real loud at the top of my lungs: WHY DON'T YOU GET YOUR TOOTH FIXED? And everyone looked at me real angry, and I looked embarrassed, and then I shouted: JUST A SUGGESTION. And everyone looked uncomfortable, and there was silence for about half an hour, and then the meeting was over, though we all said the A.A. prayer again; and then nobody would speak to me. But lots of people went to speak to the woman without the tooth, sort of like to prove that they didn't care she was missing her tooth; but then this one person came over to me, and said not to drink the punch, and he said that he agreed with me and that the woman looked awful; and that furthermore he'd been going to meetings for a long time, and that this woman had been missing her tooth for several years, and clearly had not organized herself into fixing this, and so he agreed with me wholeheartedly. And then he and I went to a hotel room and fucked, and then I tried to jump out the window, and then I went to Creedmoor for the third time. *[Looks thoughtful.]*

Have you all wondered why sexual intercourse sometimes makes you want to commit suicide? That is a universal feeling, isn't it? Or is it just me? Can I see a show of hands?

NOTES FOR THIS SPEECH:

'Mother Theresa': famous nun who set up Indian hospices; a by-word for charitable worker;

'Sally Jessy Raphael': legendary radio and television talk show host;

'AA': Alcoholics Anonymous;

'Phil Donahue': famous chat show host;

'Creedmoor': famous Creedmoor Psychiatric Center.

The author suggests that topical references (such as Mother Theresa) can be brought up to date if you wish, and you might want to change some of the strong language: See Note 3.

The end bit about going to the hotel room, and then asking for a show of hands, should come as complete surprises: **See Note 5.**

Your character is addressing the audience: **See Note 6.**

51

SISTER MARY IGNATIUS EXPLAINS IT ALL FOR YOU

Christopher Durang

FIRST PERFORMANCES	New York 1979; London 1983
AWARDS	Elizabeth Franz nominated for the *Drama Desk Award for Outstanding Actress in a Play*.
CHARACTER	Sister Mary
PLAYED BY	Elizabeth Franz [US]; Maria Aitken [UK]
CHARACTER'S AGE	over 50
CHARACTER'S TYPE	She is an old-fashioned teaching nun, much concerned with sin. She could be any age from 40 to 60.
TIME AND PLACE	1980s; a classroom in a traditional Catholic school.
SITUATION	Sister Mary is answering written questions from the children, one of whom, Thomas, is on stage with her.

Sister Mary: I'll take the next one.

[Reads.] Are you ever sorry you became a nun?

I am never sorry I became a nun.

[Reads.] It used to be a mortal sin to eat meat on Fridays, and now it isn't. Does that mean that people who ate meat on Fridays back when it was a sin are in hell? Or what?

People who ate meat on Fridays back when it was a mortal sin are indeed in hell if they did not confess the sin before they died. If they confessed it, they are not in hell, unless they did not confess some other mortal sin they committed.

People who would eat meat on Fridays back in the 50s tended to be the sort who would commit other mortal sins, so on a guess, I bet many of them *are* in hell for other sins, even if they did confess the eating of meat.

[Reads.] What exactly went on in Sodom?

[Irritated.] Who asked me this question?

[Reads.] I am an Aries. Is it a sin to follow your horoscope?

It is a sin to follow your horoscope because only God knows the future and He won't tell us. Also, we can tell that horoscopes are false because according to astrology Christ would be a Capricorn, and Capricorn people are cold, ambitious and attracted to Scorpio and Virgo, and we know that Christ was warm, loving, and not attracted to anybody. Give me a cookie, Thomas. *[He does.]* I'm going to talk about Sodom a bit. Thomas, please leave the stage. *[She talks softer.]* To answer your question, Sodom is where they committed acts of homosexuality and bestiality in the Old Testament, and God, infuriated by this, destroyed them all in one fell swoop. Modern day Sodoms are New York City, San Francisco, Amsterdam, Los Angeles, . . . well, basically anywhere where the population is over 50,000. The only reason that God has not destroyed these modern day Sodoms is that Catholic nuns and priests live in these cities, and God does not wish to destroy them. He does, however, give these people body lice and hepatitis. It's so hard to know why God allows wickedness to flourish. I guess it's because God wants man to choose goodness freely of his own free will; sometimes one wonders if free will is worth all the trouble if there's going to be so much evil and unhappiness, but God knows best, presumably. If it were up to me, I might be tempted to wipe out cities and civilizations, but luckily for New York and Amsterdam, I'm not God.

NOTES FOR THIS SPEECH:

You can always cut the section on eating meat on Fridays if you need a shorter version of the speech: See Note 2.

You are talking to the audience, as if they were small children: See Note 6.

An Irish accent would work well for this piece: See Note 7.

You can move around if you wish, or play the whole thing sitting in a chair: See Note 8.

52

HUMBLE BOY

Charlotte Jones

FIRST PERFORMANCES	London 2001; New York 2003
AWARDS	Nominated for the *Laurence Olivier Award for Best New Play*, and the *Drama Desk Award for Outstanding Play*.
	Marcia Warren **won** the *Laurence Olivier Award for Best Supporting Actress*.
CHARACTER	Mercy
PLAYED BY	Marcia Warren [UK]; Mary Beth Hurt [US]
CHARACTER'S AGE	late 50s
CHARACTER'S TYPE	The next-door neighbour, she is a petite, timid, mousy spinster; a typical Women's Institute member.
TIME AND PLACE	Now; garden of a pleasant home in the Cotswolds, England.
SITUATION	Felix has returned home for the funeral of his father James, his mother being Flora. They are all having supper in the garden, and Mercy is saying a prayer that covers all the problems of everyone at the table.

Mercy: For what we are about to receive, which none of you really want to eat but which I stayed up till two in the morning to make and I didn't even have any pimentos and had to improvise round them, may the Lord, whether you believe in Him or not, I know you don't Felix because you're a scientist so you're not allowed to and anyway I don't know if I do, because of things like James dying in the way that he did and little Felicity not having an identifiable father and the terrible things that Flora has said to me and the little fat bumblebees just dropping down dead from the sky. And I know that what James said about the finite number of heartbeats should be a comfort, but it is not. And maybe I don't have much of a life but up to now God has filled all the gaps but now there do seem to be holes that He can't fill so perhaps you are right, Flora, because even though I still do the flowers in church and my various parish duties really I would say that I was unofficially on a sabbatical from God at the moment because everything is really so unsettling and I'm sick to my heart of trying all the time, trying, trying, trying, and I don't like it, I don't like it at all, so may the Lord, even though we're not on speaking terms, make us all, and I mean all of us, truly grateful. Amen.

NOTES FOR THIS SPEECH:

'Women's Institute': conservative housewives' association in the UK (known as the WI);

'pimentos': red or green peppers.

It will be fun to identify for the audience the different people round the table, the different way you feel about each of them, and the change in you as the prayer goes on: See Note 4.

Be careful not to anticipate the interrupted thoughts: See Note 5.

Although scripted as seated, you can give yourself permission to move about as you get more emotional (and you *can* pray with your eyes open); make sure the important people you are speaking about are downstage of you: See Note 8.

53

THE RETREAT FROM MOSCOW

William Nicholson

FIRST PERFORMANCES	Chichester 1999; New York 2003
AWARDS	Nominated for the *Tony Award for Best Play*.
	Eileen Atkins nominated for the *Tony Award for Best Performance by a Leading Actress in a Play*, and the *Drama Desk Award for Outstanding Actress in a Play*.
CHARACTER	Alice
PLAYED BY	Janet Suzman [UK]; Eileen Atkins [US]
CHARACTER'S AGE	late 50s
CHARACTER'S TYPE	She is an observant Catholic, exacting and opinionated.
TIME AND PLACE	Now; the English family home of Edward and Alice.
SITUATION	She has been collecting poems for a new anthology, called *Lost Love*, and is telling her son that she had great problems getting her printer fixed.

Alice: Darling, there isn't anyone. People don't fix things any more, they throw them away.

I rang every shop in the Yellow Pages, but all they wanted to do was sell me a new one. I found a man at last who said, rather grudgingly, 'Bring it in,' so I drove all the way to this hellish industrial estate, where there was this hellish computer warehouse, and I lugged the damned machine in through one of those ferocious doors that try to crush you, and there was one little man, all alone in this vast space, sitting at a keyboard, going tick-tick-tick. No attempt to help me as I struggled in. Not a word. Not a look. After a while I said, 'I'm a customer. Aren't you supposed to serve me?' He looked up and said, 'Well?' Just, 'Well?' I said, 'My printer's not working.' I showed him the page I'd brought in to explain the problem. I'd been trying to print out a Browning poem, the one that ends –

Just when I seemed about to learn!
Where is the thread now? Off again!
The old trick! Only I discern –
Infinite passion, and the pain
Of finite hearts that yearn.

That's going into Lost Love, too. It's turning out to be by far the largest section in the anthology. Anyway, the printer had left off the first two words or so of every line, which made the poem rather modern, but not as good. The man in the warehouse said, 'That's not a printer problem. The printer's fine. It's what you're doing that's wrong. You're the problem.' He actually said it, in those very words. 'You're the problem.' 'How do you know?' I said. 'You haven't looked at the printer. You haven't even switched it on.' 'I know,' he said, 'because if a printer prints wrong, it's not the printer's fault.' 'Are you the printer's mother?' I asked him. 'Are you telling me that printers never go wrong?' 'I'm telling you,' he said. 'that if the printer's printing, then the printer's fine.' 'But it's not fine,' I said. 'It's not printing right. Well, actually, it is printing right, but it's not printing left.' He didn't have an answer to that. He went back to going tick-tick-tick. 'Excuse me,' I said. 'I'm not finished. I want you to look at my printer.' He paid me no attention whatsoever. So I picked up my printer, to take it over to where he sat, and I dropped it.

It made a kind of tinkling noise. He looked up when he heard that, and smiled a cruel little smile, and said, 'Would you like me to sell you a new printer?' I was so angry I wanted to hit him. So I said to him, 'You're the kind of man who doesn't love anybody and nobody loves you. You've got no friends, and your wife hates you, and your children never talk to you.' He looked quite surprised for a moment or two. Then he said, 'Do you know me from somewhere?'

NOTES FOR THIS SPEECH:

You could always cut the poem if you needed to shorten the piece, or if it is inappropriate to your needs: See Note 1.

Make sure that the last line comes as a surprise: See Note 5.

It may be nice to do the man's voice in a different accent: See Note 7.

54

LETTICE AND LOVAGE

Peter Shaffer

FIRST PERFORMANCES	London 1987; New York 1990
AWARDS	**Won** the *Evening Standard Theatre Award for Best Comedy*; nominated for the *Laurence Olivier Award for Best Play of the Year*, **and** the *Tony Award for Best Play*.
	Maggie Smith **won** the *Tony Award for Best Actress in a Play*; nominated for the *Laurence Olivier Award for Best Actress of the Year*.
CHARACTER	Lettice
PLAYED BY	Maggie Smith [UK and US]
CHARACTER'S AGE	50s
CHARACTER'S TYPE	She is in her middle life, passionate about history and theatre, and refuses to accept the mediocre and second rate.
TIME AND PLACE	Today; a historical mansion, England.
SITUATION	Lettice is working as a guide to Fustian House, a mid-sixteenth century building, and likes to embellish the dry tales from the past for her group tours.

Lettice: It was upon these very stairs in the reign of William and Mary, that the most *terrible* of all events connected with this house occurred – on Midsummer morning, sixteen hundred and eighty-nine.

[Warming to her tale] This day was intended to celebrate the marriage of Miss Arabella Fustian to the handsomest young lordling in the region. The

bride was a radiantly beautiful girl of eighteen – 'the catch of the County', as she was called. On the morning of her wedding her father, Sir Nicholas, stood exactly where I stand now – waiting to escort his only daughter to the church. The door of the bedchamber opened above – *[She points:]* – and out stepped this exquisite creature in a miasma of white samite. It is not hard to imagine her father staring up at her, tears welling in his old eyes – she about to descend these stairs for the last time a maiden! And then – ah, suddenly! a terrible drumming is heard! A frantic pounding along the oak gallery – and towards her, galloping at full speed, is Charger, the faithful mastiff of the family, wild with excitement at smelling the nuptial baked meats roasting in the kitchen below! In his hurtling frenzy he knocks the girl aside. She staggers – flails the air – shoots our her hand for the banister, which alas is too far from her, and *falls headlong* after the beast! . . . her lovely body rolling like a cloud down the fifteen stairs you see, until at last with one appalling jolt it comes to rest at her father's feet! . . . *[She points to the spot, at her own.]* No Mercury he, but ancient and arthritic, he stoops to touch her. Is she dead? No, the Saints be praised! Her neck is unbroken. *[A pause.]* In a dreadful echo of the gesture with which his ancestor won the family title, he catches the girl up in his arms and, watched by the agonized dog, carries her upwards to her room. A room she was never to leave again. Arabella regained consciousness, yes, but her legs, which had danced the gavotte and the coranto as no legs had ever danced them, were now twisted beneath her in mockery of the love-knots which grace the plaster ceiling above you.

By her own choice the girl immured herself in that chamber up there for life, receiving no visitors but howling incessantly the Marriage Hymn which had been specially composed for her by Henry Purcell himself! . . . The Family Chronicle records that her attendants were all likewise distorted. I quote it for you. 'The wretched lady would employ as domestics only those who were deformed in the legs and haunches: knotted women, hunchbacks, swivel-hips, and such as had warpage and osseous misalignment of the limbs.' Cripples of all shapes clawed their way daily up this staircase, which was now known no longer as The Staircase of Ennoblement, but the *Staircase of Wound and Woe!* This name it has retained ever since.

NOTES FOR THIS SPEECH:

'miasma': poisonous vapour; *Lettice* probably thought it meant 'cloud';

'samite': heavy medieval silk with gold threads, not easy to billow out as a 'miasma';

'Mercury': messenger of the Gods, so Sir Nicholas moved quickly;

'warpage': twisted out of shape;

'osseous': bony

You may find this a bit long, and could trim it by cutting the last paragraph, or making internal cuts: **See Note 2.**

Feel free to change any of the obscure words: **See Note 3.**

It may be tempting to put on a 'character' voice for this piece. However, a naturally unusual quality might be amusing and add to the self-indulgence required. Lettice clearly likes the sound of her own voice!: **See Note 7.**

Make sure that some of the invisible group listening to you are downstage and on both sides of you; and the staircase you are describing could also be downstage, where the audience is: **See Note 8.**

INDEX OF PLAYWRIGHTS

INDEX OF PLAYS

INDEX OF ACTORS

AWARD LIST FROM 1980 TO 2006

(* = winner)

In the US the nominations are taken from the *Tony Awards for Best Play*; and the *Drama Desk Awards for Outstanding Play/Outstanding New Play*, together with the winner of the *Pulitzer Prize for Drama*.

In the UK the nominations are taken from the *Evening Standard Theatre Awards for Best Play* and *Best Comedy*; and the *Laurence Olivier Awards for Best Play of the Year/Best New Play*, and *Best Comedy of the Year/Best Comedy/Best New Comedy*.

(In order to put the plays in their proper groupings, the year is for the period that the award covered, not necessarily the year in which the award was given.)

1980

The Pulitzer Prize for Drama:
Crimes of the Heart – Beth Henley

Tony Award nominations for Best Play:
A Lesson from Aloes – Athol Fugard
A Life – Hugh Leonard
*Amadeus – Peter Shaffer
Fifth of July – Lanford Wilson

Drama Desk Award nominations for Outstanding New Play:
*Amadeus – Peter Shaffer
Crimes of the Heart – Beth Henley
Fifth of July – Lanford Wilson
Mass Appeal – Bill C. Davis

Evening Standard Theatre Award for Best Play:
The Dresser – Ronald Harwood

Evening Standard Theatre Award for Best Comedy:
Make and Break – Michael Frayn

Laurence Olivier Award nominations for Best Play of the Year:
A Lesson from Aloes – Athol Fugard
Duet for One – Tom Kempinski
The Dresser – Ronald Harwood
*The Life and Adventures of Nicholas Nickleby – David Edgar, from the novel
    by Charles Dickens

Laurence Olivier Award nominations for Best Comedy of the Year:
Born in the Gardens – Peter Nichols
*Educating Rita – Willy Russell
Make and Break – Michael Frayn
Sisterly Feelings – Alan Ayckbourn

1981

The Pulitzer Prize for Drama:
A Soldier's Play – Charles Fuller

Tony Award nominations for Best Play:
Crimes of the Heart – Beth Henley
Master Harold and the Boys – Athol Fugard
The Dresser – Ronald Harwood
*The Life and Adventures of Nicholas Nickleby – David Edgar, from the novel
    by Charles Dickens

Drama Desk Award nominations for Outstanding New Play:
A Soldier's Play – Charles Fuller
The Dance and the Railroad – David Henry Hwang
Family Devotions – David Henry Hwang
Grown Ups – Jules Feiffer
*Master Harold and the Boys – Athol Fugard
The Dining Room – A.R. Gurney
Torch Song Trilogy – Harvey Fierstein

Evening Standard Theatre Award for Best Play:
Passion Play – Peter Nichols

Evening Standard Theatre Award for Best Comedy:
Goose Pimples – Mike Leigh

Laurence Olivier Award nominations for Best Play of the Year:
*Children of a Lesser God – Mark Medoff
Passion Play – Peter Nichols
Quartermaine's Terms – Simon Gray
Translations – Brian Friel

Laurence Olivier Award nominations for Best Comedy of the Year:
Anyone for Denis? – John Wells
Can't Pay? Won't Pay! – Dario Fo, translated by Lino Pertile, Bill Conville, Robert
    Walker
On the Razzle – Tom Stoppard
*Steaming – Nell Dunn

1982

The Pulitzer Prize for Drama:
'Night Mother: A Play – Marsha Norman

Tony Award nominations for Best Play:
Angels Fall – Lanford Wilson
'Night Mother: A Play – Marsha Norman
Plenty – David Hare
*Torch Song Trilogy – Harvey Fierstein

Drama Desk Award nominations for Outstanding New Play:
Brighton Beach Memoirs – Neil Simon
Edmund – David Mamet
Extremities – William Mastrosimone
Geniuses – Jonathan Reynolds
*Torch Song Trilogy – Harvey Fierstein
True West – Sam Shepard

Evening Standard Theatre Award for Best Play:
The Real Thing – Tom Stoppard

Evening Standard Theatre Award for Best Comedy:
Noises Off – Michael Frayn

Laurence Olivier Award nominations for Best Play of the Year:
84 Charing Cross Road – James Roose Evans, from the book by Helene Hanff
*Another Country – Julian Mitchell
Our Friends in the North – Peter Flannery

Laurence Olivier Award nominations for Best Comedy of the Year:
Key for Two – Dave Freeman, John Chapman
*Noises Off – Michael Frayn
Season's Greetings – Alan Ayckbourn
Trafford Tanzi – Claire Luckham

1983

The Pulitzer Prize for Drama:
Glengarry Glen Ross – David Mamet

Tony Award nominations for Best Play:
Glengarry Glen Ross – David Mamet
Noises Off – Michael Frayn
Play Memory – Joanna Glass
*The Real Thing – Tom Stoppard

Drama Desk Award nominations for Outstanding New Play:
A Private View – Vaclav Havel
And a Nightingale Sang – C.P. Taylor
Glengarry Glen Ross – David Mamet
Isn't It Romantic – Wendy Wasserstein
Noises Off – Michael Frayn
*The Real Thing – Tom Stoppard

Evening Standard Theatre Award for Best Play:
Master Harold and the Boys – Athol Fugard

Evening Standard Theatre Award for Best Comedy:
Tales from Hollywood – Christopher Hampton

Laurence Olivier Award nominations for Best Play of the Year:
A Pack of Lies – Hugh Whitemore
*Glengarry Glen Ross – David Mamet
Tales from Hollywood – Christopher Hampton
The Slab Boys – John Byrne

Laurence Olivier Award nominations for Best Comedy of the Year:
Beethoven's Tenth – Peter Ustinov
*Daisy Pulls It Off – Denise Deegan
Run for Your Wife – Ray Cooney
Woza Albert! – Barney Simon, Percy Mtwa, Mbongeni Ngema

1984

The Pulitzer Prize for Drama:
Sunday in the Park with George – Stephen Sondheim and James Lapine

Tony Award nominations for Best Play:
As Is – William M. Hoffman
*Biloxi Blues – Neil Simon
Hurlyburly – David Rabe
Ma Rainey's Black Bottom – August Wilson

Drama Desk Award nominations for Outstanding New Play:
*As Is – William F. Hoffman
Biloxi Blues – Neil Simon
Digby – Joseph Dougherty
Ma Rainey's Black Bottom – August Wilson

Evening Standard Theatre Award for Best Play:
Benefactors – Michael Frayn

Evening Standard Theatre Award for Best Comedy:
Stepping Out – Richard Harris

Laurence Olivier Award nominations for Best Play of the Year:
*Benefactors – Michael Frayn
Master Harold and the Boys – Athol Fugard
Poppie Nongena – Elsa Joubert, Sandra Kotze
Rat in the Skull – Ron Hutchinson

Laurence Olivier Award nominations for Best Comedy of the Year:
Gymslip Vicar – Cliffhanger Theatre Company
Intimate Exchanges – Alan Ayckbourn
Two Into One – Ray Cooney
*Up 'N' Under – John Godber

1985

The Pulitzer Prize for Drama:
Not awarded

Tony Award nominations for Best Play:
Benefactors – Michael Frayn
Blood Knot – Athol Fugard
*I'm Not Rappaport – Herb Gardner
The House of Blue Leaves – John Guare

Drama Desk Award nominations for Outstanding New Play:
*A Lie of the Mind – Sam Shepard
Aunt Dan and Lemon – Wallace Shawn
Benefactors – Michael Frayn
Execution of Justice – Emily Mann
Precious Sons – George Furth
The Marriage of Bette and Boo – Christopher Durang

Evening Standard Theatre Award for Best Play:
Pravda – Howard Brenton, David Hare

Evening Standard Theatre Award for Best Comedy:
A Chorus of Disapproval – Alan Ayckbourn

Laurence Olivier Award nominations for Best Play of the Year:

Doomsday – Tony Harrison

*Red Noses – Peter Barnes

The Road to Mecca – Athol Fugard

Torch Song Trilogy – Harvey Fierstein

Laurence Olivier Award nominations for Best Comedy of the Year:

*A Chorus of Disapproval – Alan Ayckbourn

Bouncers – John Godber

Love's Labours Lost – William Shakespeare

Pravda – Howard Brenton, David Hare

1986

The Pulitzer Prize for Drama:

Fences – August Wilson

Tony Award nominations for Best Play:

Broadway Bound – Neil Simon

Coastal Disturbances – Tina Howe

*Fences – August Wilson

Les Liaisons Dangereuses – Christopher Hampton, from the novel by Choderlos de Laclos

Drama Desk Award nominations for Outstanding New Play:

Broadway Bound – Neil Simon

Driving Miss Daisy – Alfred Uhry

*Fences – August Wilson

Les Liaisons Dangereuses – Christopher Hampton, from the novel by Choderlos de Laclos

North Shore Fish – Israel Horovitz

The Common Pursuit – Simon Gray

Wild Honey – Michael Frayn

Evening Standard Theatre Award for Best Play:

Les Liaisons Dangereuses – Christopher Hampton, from the novel by Choderlos de Laclos

A Month of Sundays – Bob Larbey

Laurence Olivier Award nominations for Best Play of the Year:
*Les Liaisons Dangereuses – Christopher Hampton, from the novel by
    Choderlos de Laclos
Ourselves Alone – Anne Devlin
The American Clock – Arthur Miller
The Normal Heart – Larry Kramer

Laurence Olivier Award nominations for Best Comedy of the Year:
A Midsummer Night's Dream – William Shakespeare
Lend Me a Tenor – Ken Ludwig
The Merry Wives of Windsor – William Shakespeare
*When We Are Married – J.B. Priestley

1987

The Pulitzer Prize for Drama:
Driving Miss Daisy – Alfred Uhry

Tony Award nominations for Best Play:
A Walk in the Woods – Lee Blessing
Joe Turner's Come and Gone – August Wilson
*M. Butterfly – David Henry Hwang
Speed the Plow – David Mamet

Drama Desk Award nominations for Outstanding New Play:
Boys' Life – Howard Korder
Joe Turner's Come and Gone – August Wilson
*M. Butterfly – David Henry Hwang
Speed the Plow – David Mamet
The Road to Mecca – Athol Fugard
Women in Mind – Alan Ayckbourn

Evening Standard Theatre Award for Best Play:
A Small Family Business – Alan Ayckbourn

Evening Standard Theatre Award for Best Comedy:
Serious Money – Caryl Churchill

Laurence Olivier Award nominations for Best Play of the Year:
A Lie of the Mind – Sam Shepard
Lettice and Lovage – Peter Shaffer
Sarcophagus – Vladimir Gubaryev
*Serious Money – Caryl Churchill

Laurence Olivier Award nominations for Best Comedy of the Year:
A Midsummer Night's Dream – William Shakespeare
Groucho – Arthur Marx, Robert Fisher
*Three Men on a Horse – John Cecil Holm, George Abbott
Twelfth Night – William Shakespeare

1988

The Pulitzer Prize for Drama:
The Heidi Chronicles – Wendy Wasserstein

Tony Award nominations for Best Play:
Largely New York – Bill Irwin
Lend Me a Tenor – Ken Ludwig
Shirley Valentine – Willy Russell
*The Heidi Chronicles – Wendy Wasserstein

Drama Desk Award nominations for Outstanding New Play:
Only Kidding – Jim Geoghan
Reckless – Craig Lucas
Shirley Valentine – Willy Russell
The Cocktail Hour – A.R. Gurney
The Film Society – Jon Robin Baitz
*The Heidi Chronicles – Wendy Wasserstein

Evening Standard Theatre Award for Best Play:
Aristocrats – Brian Friel

Evening Standard Theatre Award for Best Comedy:
Lettice and Lovage – Peter Shaffer

Laurence Olivier Award nominations for Best Play of the Year:
A Walk in the Woods – Lee Blessing
Mrs. Klein – Nicholas Wright
*Our Country's Good – Timberlake Wertenbaker
The Secret Rapture – David Hare

Laurence Olivier Award nominations for Best Comedy of the Year:
Henceforward – Alan Ayckbourn
Separation – Tom Kempinski
*Shirley Valentine – Willy Russell
The Common Pursuit – Simon Gray

1989

The Pulitzer Prize for Drama:
The Piano Lesson – August Wilson

Tony Award nominations for Best Play:
Lettice and Lovage – Peter Shaffer
Prelude to a Kiss – Craig Lucas
*The Grapes of Wrath – Frank Galati, from the novel by John Steinbeck
The Piano Lesson – August Wilson

Drama Desk Award nominations for Outstanding New Play:
Prelude to a Kiss – Craig Lucas
Some Americans Abroad – Richard Nelson
The Lisbon Traviata – Terrence McNally
*The Piano Lesson – August Wilson
The Secret Rapture – David Hare

Evening Standard Theatre Award for Best Play:
Ghetto – Joshua Sobol

Evening Standard Theatre Award for Best Comedy:
Henceforward – Alan Ayckbourn

Laurence Olivier Award nominations for Best New Play:
Ghetto – Joshua Sobol
Man of the Moment – Alan Ayckbourn
*Racing Demon – David Hare
Shadowlands – William Nicholson

Laurence Olivier Award nominations for Comedy of the Year:
*Single Spies – Alan Bennett
Some Americans Abroad – Richard Nelson
Steel Magnolias – Robert Harling
Jeffrey Bernard is Unwell – Keith Waterhouse

1990

The Pulitzer Prize for Drama:
Lost in Yonkers – Neil Simon

Tony Award nominations for Best Play:
*Lost in Yonkers – Neil Simon
Our Country's Good – Timberlake Wertenbaker
Shadowlands – William Nicholson
Six Degrees of Separation – John Guare

Drama Desk Award nominations for Outstanding New Play:
La Bête – David Hirson
*Lost in Yonkers – Neil Simon
Six Degrees of Separation – John Guare
The Wash – Philip Kan Gotanda

Evening Standard Theatre Award for Best Play:
Shadowlands – William Nicholson

Evening Standard Theatre Award for Best Comedy:
Man of the Moment – Alan Ayckbourn
Jeffrey Bernard is Unwell – Keith Waterhouse

Laurence Olivier Award nominations for Best New Play:
*Dancing at Lughnasa – Brian Friel
Singer – Peter Flannery
The Trackers of Oxyrhynchus – Tony Harrison
White Chameleon – Christopher Hampton

Laurence Olivier Award nominations for Best Comedy:
Gasping – Ben Elton
*Out of Order – Ray Cooney

1991

The Pulitzer Prize for Drama:
The Kentucky Cycle – Robert Schenkkan

Tony Award nominations for Best Play:
*Dancing at Lughnasa – Brian Friel
Four Baboons Adoring the Sun – John Guare
Two Shakespearean Actors – Richard Nelson
Two Trains Running – August Wilson

Drama Desk Award nominations for Outstanding New Play:
A Small Family Business – Alan Ayckbourn
Dancing at Lughnasa – Brian Friel
Lips Together, Teeth Apart – Terrence McNally
Mad Forest – Caryl Churchill
*Marvin's Room – Scott McPherson
Sight Unseen – Donald Margulies

Evening Standard Theatre Award for Best Play:
Dancing at Lughnasa – Brian Friel

Evening Standard Theatre Award for Best Comedy:
Kvetch – Steven Berkoff

Laurence Olivier Award nominations for Best New Play:
Angels in America: Millennium Approaches – Tony Kushner
*Death and the Maiden – Ariel Dorfman
The Madness of George III – Alan Bennett
Three Birds Alighting on a Field – Timberlake Wertenbaker

Laurence Olivier Award nominations for Best Comedy:
An Evening with Gary Lineker – Arthur Smith, Chris England
It's Ralph – Hugh Whitemore
*La Bête – David Hirson

1992

The Pulitzer Prize for Drama:
Angels in America: Millennium Approaches – Tony Kushner

Tony Award nominations for Best Play:
*Angels in America: Millennium Approaches – Tony Kushner
Someone Who'll Watch Over Me – Frank McGuinness
The Sisters Rosensweig – Wendy Wasserstein
The Song of Jacob Zulu – Tug Yourgrau

Drama Desk Award nominations for Outstanding New Play:
*Angels in America: Millennium Approaches – Tony Kushner
Jeffrey – Paul Rudnick
Joined at the Head – Catherine Butterfield
Oleanna – David Mamet
The Sisters Rosensweig – Wendy Wasserstein
Three Hotels – Jon Robin Baitz

Evening Standard Theatre Award for Best Play:
Angels in America: Millennium Approaches – Tony Kushner

Evening Standard Theatre Award for Best Comedy:
The Rise and Fall of Little Voice – Jim Cartwright

Laurence Olivier Award nominations for Best New Play:

*Six Degrees of Separation – John Guare

Someone Who'll Watch Over Me – Frank McGuinness

The Gift of the Gorgon – Peter Shaffer

The Street of Crocodiles – Théâtre de Complicité, from stories by Bruno Sculz

Laurence Olivier Award nominations for Best Comedy:

Lost in Yonkers – Neil Simon

On the Piste – John Godber

*The Rise and Fall of Little Voice – Jim Cartwright

1993

The Pulitzer Prize for Drama:

Three Tall Women – Edward Albee

Tony Award nominations for Best Play:

*Angels in America: Perestroika – Tony Kushner

Broken Glass – Arthur Miller

The Kentucky Cycle – Robert Schenkkan

Twilight: Los Angeles, 1992 – Anna Deavere Smith

Drama Desk Award nominations for Outstanding Play:

*Angels in America: Perestroika – Tony Kushner

All in the Timing – David Ives

The Kentucky Cycle – Robert Schenkkan

The Lights – Howard Korder

Pterodactyls – Nicky Silver

Evening Standard Theatre Award for Best Play:

Arcadia – Tom Stoppard

Evening Standard Theatre Award for Best Comedy:

Jamais Vu – Ken Campbell

Laurence Olivier Award nominations for Best New Play:
Angels in America: Perestroika – Tony Kushner
*Arcadia – Tom Stoppard
Oleanna – David Mamet
The Last Yankee – Arthur Miller

Laurence Olivier Award nominations for Best Comedy:
April in Paris – John Godber
*Hysteria – Terry Johnson
The Life of Stuff – Simon Donald
Time of My Life – Alan Ayckbourn

1994

The Pulitzer Prize for Drama:
The Young Man from Atlanta – Horton Foote

Tony Award nominations for Best Play:
Arcadia – Tom Stoppard
Having Our Say – Emily Mann
Indiscretions – Jean Cocteau, translated by Jeremy Sams
*Love! Valour! Compassion! – Terrence McNally

Drama Desk Award nominations for Outstanding Play:
Arcadia – Tom Stoppard
*Love! Valour! Compassion! – Terrence McNally
Missing Persons – Craig Lucas
Raised in Captivity – Nicky Silver
SubUrbia – Eric Bogosian
The Cryptogram – David Mamet

Evening Standard Theatre Award for Best Play:
Three Tall Women – Edward Albee

Evening Standard Theatre Award for Best Comedy:
My Night with Reg – Kevin Elyot

Laurence Olivier Award nominations for Best New Play:
900 Oneonta – David Beaird
*Broken Glass – Arthur Miller
Dealer's Choice – Patrick Marber
Three Tall Women – Edward Albee

Laurence Olivier Award nominations for Best Comedy:
Beautiful Thing – Jonathan Harvey
Dead Funny – Terry Johnson
*My Night with Reg – Kevin Elyot
Neville's Island – Tim Firth

1995

The Pulitzer Prize for Drama:
Rent – Jonathan Larson

Tony Award nominations for Best Play:
Buried Child – Sam Shepard
*Master Class – Terrence McNally
Racing Demon – David Hare
Seven Guitars – August Wilson

Drama Desk Award nominations for Outstanding Play:
*Master Class – Terrence McNally
Molly Sweeney – Brian Friel
Seven Guitars – August Wilson
Sylvia – A.R. Gurney
The Model Apartment – Donald Margulies
Valley Song – Athol Fugard

Evening Standard Theatre Award for Best Play:
Pentecost – David Edgar

Evening Standard Theatre Award for Best Comedy:
Dealer's Choice – Patrick Marber

1996

Laurence Olivier Award nominations for Best New Play:
Blinded by the Sun – Stephen Poliakoff
*Stanley – Pam Gems
The Beauty Queen of Leenane – Martin McDonagh
The Herbal Bed – Peter Whelan

Laurence Olivier Award nominations for Best Comedy:
*Art – Yasmina Reza, translated by Christopher Hampton
Laughter on the 23rd Floor – Neil Simon
The Complete Works of William Shakespeare (abridged) – A. Long, D. Singer,
    J. Winfield

1997

The Pulitzer Prize for Drama:
How I Learned to Drive – Paula Vogel

Tony Award nominations for Best Play:
*Art – Yasmina Reza, translated by Christopher Hampton
Freak – John Leguizamo
Golden Child – David Henry Hwang
The Beauty Queen of Leenane – Martin McDonagh

Drama Desk Award nominations for Outstanding Play:
Art – Yasmina Reza, translated by Christopher Hampton
As Bees in Honey Drown – Douglas Carter Beane
Collected Stories – Donald Margulies
Side Man – Warren Leight
*The Beauty Queen of Leenane – Martin McDonagh
Three Days of Rain – Richard Greenberg

Evening Standard Theatre Award for Best Play:
The Invention of Love – Tom Stoppard

Evening Standard Theatre Award for Best Comedy:
Closer – Patrick Marber

Laurence Olivier Award nominations for Best New Play:

Amy's View – David Hare

*Closer – Patrick Marber

Hurlyburly – David Rabe

The Invention of Love – Tom Stoppard

Tom and Clem – Stephen Churchett

Laurence Olivier Award nominations for Best New Comedy:

A Skull in Connemara – Martin McDonagh

East is East – Ayub Khan-Din

*Popcorn – Ben Elton

1998

The Pulitzer Prize for Drama:

Wit – Margaret Edson

Tony Award nominations for Best Play:

Closer – Patrick Marber

Not About Nightingales – Tennessee Williams

*Side Man – Warren Leight

The Lonesome West – Martin McDonagh

Drama Desk Award nominations for Outstanding Play:

Betty's Summer Vacation – Christopher Durang

Closer – Patrick Marber

Not About Nightingales – Tennessee Williams

Snakebit – David Marshall Grant

The Ride Down Mount Morgan – Arthur Miller

*Wit – Margaret Edson

Evening Standard Theatre Award for Best Play:

Copenhagen – Michael Frayn

Evening Standard Theatre Award for Best Comedy:

No award

Laurence Olivier Award nominations for Best New Play:
Copenhagen – Michael Frayn
The Blue Room – David Hare
The Unexpected Man – Yasmina Reza, translated by Christopher Hampton
*The Weir – Conor McPherson

Laurence Olivier Award nominations for Best New Comedy:
Alarms and Excursions – Michael Frayn
*Cleo, Camping, Emmanuelle and Dick – Terry Johnson
Love upon the Throne – Patrick Barlow
Things We Do For Love – Alan Ayckbourn

1999

The Pulitzer Prize for Drama:
Dinner With Friends – Donald Margulies

Tony Award nominations for Best Play:
*Copenhagen – Michael Frayn
Dirty Blonde – Claudia Shear
The Ride Down Mount Morgan – Arthur Miller
True West – Sam Shepard

Drama Desk Award nominations for Outstanding New Play:
Contact – Frank Gilroy
*Copenhagen – Michael Frayn
Dinner with Friends – Donald Margulies
Dirty Blonde – Claudia Shear
Jitney – August Wilson
The Tale of the Allergist's Wife – Charles Busch

Evening Standard Theatre Award for Best Play:
No award

Evening Standard Theatre Award for Best Comedy:
No award

Laurence Olivier Award nominations for Best New Play:
*Goodnight Children Everywhere – Richard Nelson
Perfect Days – Liz Lochhead
Rose – Martin Sherman
The Lady in the Van – Alan Bennett
Three Days of Rain – Richard Greenberg

Laurence Olivier Award nominations for Best New Comedy:
Comic Potential – Alan Ayckbourn
Quartet – Ronald Harwood
*The Memory of Water – Shelagh Stephenson

2000

The Pulitzer Prize for Drama:
Proof – David Auburn

Tony Award nominations for Best Play:
King Hedley II – August Wilson
*Proof – David Auburn
The Invention of Love – Tom Stoppard
The Tale of the Allergist's Wife – Charles Busch

Drama Desk Award nominations for Outstanding Play:
Boy Gets Girl – Rebecca Gilman
Comic Potential – Alan Ayckbourn
Lobby Hero – Kenneth Lonergan
*Proof – David Auburn
The Invention of Love – Tom Stoppard
The Unexpected Man – Yasmina Reza, translated by Christopher Hampton

Evening Standard Theatre Award for Best Play:
Blue/Orange – Joe Penhall

Evening Standard Theatre Award for Best Comedy:
Stones in His Pockets – Marie Jones

Laurence Olivier Award nominations for Best New Play:
*Blue/Orange – Joe Penhall
Dolly West's Kitchen – Frank McGuinness
Life x 3 – Yasmina Reza, translated by Christopher Hampton
My Zinc Bed – David Hare

Laurence Olivier Award nominations for Best New Comedy:
Cooking with Elvis – Lee Hall
House/Garden – Alan Ayckbourn
Peggy for You – Alan Plater
*Stones in His Pockets – Marie Jones

2001

The Pulitzer Prize for Drama:
Topdog/Underdog – Suzan-Lori Parks

Tony Award nominations for Best Play:
Fortune's Fool – by Ivan Turgenev, adapted by Mike Poulton
Metamorphoses – Mary Zimmerman
*The Goat or Who Is Sylvia? – Edward Albee
Topdog/Underdog – Suzan-Lori Parks

Drama Desk Award nominations for Outstanding Play:
Franny's Way – Richard Nelson
*Metamorphoses – Mary Zimmerman
*The Goat or Who Is Sylvia? – Edward Albee
The Shape of Things – Neil LaBute
Thief River – Lee Blessing
Topdog/Underdog – Suzan-Lori Parks

Evening Standard Theatre Award nominations for Best Play:
*The Far Side of the Moon – Robert Lepage
Mouth to Mouth – Kevin Elyot
The Shape of Things – Neil LaBute

Evening Standard Theatre Award nominations for Best Comedy:
Caught in the Net – Ray Cooney
*Feelgood – Alistair Beaton
Life x 3 – Yasmina Reza , translated by Christopher Hampton

Laurence Olivier Award nominations for Best New Play:
Boy Gets Girl – Rebecca Gilman
Gagarin Way – Gregory Burke
Humble Boy – Charlotte Jones
*Jitney – August Wilson
Mouth to Mouth – Kevin Elyot

Laurence Olivier Award nominations for Best New Comedy:
Boston Marriage – David Mamet
Caught in the Net – Ray Cooney
Feelgood – Alistair Beaton
*The Play What I Wrote – Hamish McColl, Sean Foley, Eddie Braben

2002

The Pulitzer Prize for Drama:
Anna in the Tropics – Nilo Cruz

Tony Award nominations for Best Play:
Enchanted April – Matthew Barber
Say Goodnight, Gracie – Rupert Holmes
*Take Me Out – Richard Greenberg
Vincent in Brixton – Nicholas Wright

Drama Desk Award nominations for Outstanding Play:
Buicks – Julian Sheppard
Our Lady of 121st Street – Stephen Adly Guirgis
Peter and Vandy – Jay DiPietro
*Take Me Out – Richard Greenberg
Talking Heads – Alan Bennett
Yellowman – Dael Orlandersmith

Evening Standard Theatre Award nominations for Best Play:
*A Number – Caryl Churchill
The Lieutenant of Inishmore – Martin McDonagh
The York Realist – Peter Gill

Laurence Olivier Award nominations for Best New Play:
Jesus Hopped the 'A' Train – Stephen Adly Guirgis
The Coast of Utopia – Voyage, Shipwreck, Salvage – Tom Stoppard
The York Realist – Peter Gill
*Vincent in Brixton – Nicholas Wright

Laurence Olivier Award nominations for Best New Comedy:
Damsels in Distress – Roleplay – Alan Ayckbourn
Dinner – Moira Buffini
Lobby Hero – Kenneth Lonergan
*The Lieutenant of Inishmore – Martin McDonagh

2003

The Pulitzer Prize for Drama:
I Am My Own Wife – Doug Wright

Tony Award nominations for Best Play:
Anna in the Tropics – Nilo Cruz
Frozen – Bryony Lavery
*I Am My Own Wife – Doug Wright
The Retreat from Moscow – William Nicholson

Drama Desk Award nominations for Outstanding Play:
Humble Boy – Charlotte Jones
*I Am My Own Wife – Doug Wright
Moby Dick – Julian Rad
The Beard of Avon – Amy Freed
The Distance from Here – Neil LaBute
The Tricky Part – Martin Moran

Evening Standard Theatre Award nominations for Best Play:
*Democracy – Michael Frayn
After Mrs Rochester – Polly Teale
Fallout – Roy Williams

Laurence Olivier Award nominations for Best New Play:
Democracy – Michael Frayn
Elmina's Kitchen – Kwame Kwei-Armah
Hitchcock Blonde – Terry Johnson
*The Pillowman – Martin McDonagh

2004

The Pulitzer Prize for Drama:
Doubt, A Parable – John Patrick Shanley

Tony Award nominations for Best Play:
Democracy – Michael Frayn
*Doubt, A Parable – John Patrick Shanley
Gem of the Ocean – August Wilson
The Pillowman – Martin McDonagh

Drama Desk Award nominations for Outstanding Play:
Democracy – Michael Frayn
*Doubt, A Parable – John Patrick Shanley
Pentecost – David Edgar
The Pillowman – Martin McDonagh
Sailor's Song – John Patrick Shanley
Sin (A Cardinal Deposed) – Michael Murphy

Evening Standard Theatre Award nominations for Best Play:
The Goat or Who is Sylvia? – Edward Albee
*The History Boys – Alan Bennett
The Pillowman – Martin McDonagh

Laurence Olivier Award nominations for Best New Play:

By the Bog of Cats – Marina Carr

Festen – David Eldridge, from the film and play by Thomas Vinterberg, Morgens Rukov, Bo hr. Hansen

The Goat or Who Is Sylvia? – Edward Albee

*The History Boys – Alan Bennett

2005

The Pulitzer Prize for Drama:
No award

Tony Award nominations for Best Play:

*The History Boys – Alan Bennett

The Lieutenant of Inishmore – Martin McDonagh

Rabbit Hole – David Lindsay-Abaire

Shining City – Conor McPherson

Drama Desk Award nominations for Outstanding Play:

*The History Boys – Alan Bennett

Stuff Happens – David Hare

No Foreigners Beyond this Point – Warren Leight

The Lieutenant of Inishmore – Martin McDonagh

Dedication or the Stuff of Dreams – Terrence McNally

The Pavilion – Craig Wright

Evening Standard Theatre Award nominations for Best Play:

2000 Years – Mike Leigh

Bloody Sunday – Richard Norton-Taylor

Harvest – Richard Bean

*The Home Place – Brian Friel

Laurence Olivier Award nominations for Best New Play:

Coram Boy – Helen Edmundson, from the novel by Jamila Gavin

Harvest – Richard Bean

*On the Shore of the Wide World – Simon Stephens

Paul – Howard Brenton

Laurence Olivier Award nominations for Best New Comedy:
Glorious! – Peter Quilter
*Heroes – Gérald Sibleyras, translated by Tom Stoppard
Shoot the Crow – Owen McCafferty

2006

The Pulitzer Prize for Drama:
Rabbit Hole – David Lindsay-Abaire

Tony Award nominations for Best Play:
The Little Dog Laughed – Douglas Carter Beane
Frost/Nixon – Peter Morgan
*The Coast of Utopia – Tom Stoppard
Radio Golf – August Wilson

Drama Desk Award nominations for Outstanding Play:
Blackbird – David Harrower
Some Men – Terrence McNally
Frost/Nixon – Peter Morgan
*The Coast of Utopia – Tom Stoppard
The Accomplices – Bernard Weinraub
Radio Golf – August Wilson

Evening Standard Theatre Award nominations for Best Play:
Frost/Nixon – Peter Morgan
*Rock 'N' Roll – Tom Stoppard
The Seafarer – Conor McPherson

Laurence Olivier Award nominations for Best New Play:
*Blackbird – David Harrower
Frost/Nixon – Peter Morgan
Rock 'N' Roll – Tom Stoppard
The Seafarer – Conor McPherson

Laurence Olivier Award nominations for Best New Comedy:
*The 39 Steps – Patrick Barlow, from the novel by John Buchan
Don Juan in Soho – Patrick Marber, from the play by Molière
Love Song – John Kolvenbach